WATCH
YOUR
BACK

RICHARD ALLEN

First published in Great Britain as a softback original in 2022

Copyright © Richard Allen

The moral right of this author has been asserted.

Editing, design, typesetting and publishing by UK Book Publishing

www.ukbookpublishing.com

ISBN: 978-1-915338-71-6

DEDICATION

I dedicate this book to my *Aunty May* who rescued me at the age of 16 and to my wife *Gwen* who joined Aunty May in the task in 1953 continuing on with the excellent work throughout the following 66 years.

A sincere thank you to both.

Richard

ACKNOWLEDGEMENTS

To: *John REDMAN* former R.M.P. Now in New Zealand
and *Bob EGGELTON*, Editor of Royal Military Police Old Comrades
Link Up Newsletter.

CONTENTS

PROFILE OF RICHARD GEORGE ALLEN

Born 25.9.1931 at Hastings, East Sussex. Educated at St. Bartholomew's Grammar School, Newbury, Berkshire whilst residing in well known 'Racing Village', namely East Ilsley, Berkshire.

National Service: Corps of Royal Military Police – achieved rank of Sergeant. (Two years plus three years on the Supplementary Reserve.)

Berkshire Constabulary:

- 1948-1950 Cadet-Newbury and Wokingham. 1952-1957 Constable at Ascot. 1957-1961 Constable at Bracknell. 1961-1962 Sergeant, Abingdon. 1962-1964 Sergeant, Administration, Force HQ, Sulhamstead.
- 1964-1967 Sergeant i/c Wallingford Section 1967-1968 Inspector i/c Woodley Sub-Division.

Thames Valley Police:

- 1968-1972 Chief Inspector i/c Admin, Bracknell Division. 1972-1973 Chief Inspector – 2i/c Force Inspection Team.
- 1973-1974 Superintendent-Force Training Officer/ Commandant Force Training Centre, Sulhamstead. Force wide responsibility
- 1974-1977 Superintendent 2i/c, Slough Division. Responsibility for East Berkshire.

- 1977-1982 Chief Superintendent/Divisional Commander. Traffic Division. Force wide responsibility. During this period carried out duties of Acting Assistant Chief Constable, Operations for two Periods of six months.
- 1982-1984 Divisional Commander, Banbury Division.

Ministry of Defence: 1985-1995 HEO Civil Service. (PVIO -RAF P & SS)

Ascot Racecourse Authority: During time in Police Service was closely involved with liaison with Ascot Racecourse.

Staff re 'Operational Matters' at all levels.

1990-1997 Assistant Raceday Manager/Race-Day Manager Paddock 1997-2000 Race-day Manager –Tattersalls, Silver Ring and all Turnstiles.

2003-2004 Controller Royal Box/Royal Liaison Officer.

Cheltenham Racing Festival: 1997-2005 Weighing Room/Jockeys Security.

Henley Royal Regatta 1999, 2000, 2001 Race-Day Security Manager.

Guards Polo Club: 1991-2009 Steward Royal Box. 2009-2011 Head Steward – Royal Box.

Outside interests: Rotary International 1966-2000. (Member of Wallingford, Bracknell, Caversham, Slough, Oxford North (twice) and

Windrush Valley (Past President) Clubs during period and involved in numerous projects, e.g. Joint Chairman (with Round Table) Bracknell Show, regularly driving mini buses for British Red Cross and other organisations, Chairman, Cliveden Band Concert Committee, Chairman of Committees for Glen Miller Evening, Oxford Town Hall, Grenadier Guards Band Concert, Blenheim Palace (with Army Benevolent Fund). Kidlington and District Probus Club (Past President). Past President of National Association of Advanced Motorists, Thames Valley Branch. Past President of Thames Valley Police Clay Pigeon Club. Past Secretary of Thames Valley Police Band. Founding Secretary of Thames Valley Police Southern Region Officers Mess. Thames Valley Police H.Q. Officers Mess (P.M.C.,1977/78/79).

Richard. G. ALLEN. 31st March, 2016.

RECOLLECTIONS OF A FORMER PUPIL AND ONLY CHILD OF A HEAD TEACHER - EAST ILSLEY COUNCIL SCHOOL

1932 TO 1948

My father, George Thomas ALLEN (known as Tom or Tommy), was born at Barkham, Berkshire on 28th April 1901, the family moving to Highgrove, High Street, Crowthorne, Berkshire in 1902. Whilst attending Crowthorne Church of England School he obtained one of nine scholarships in Berkshire, which enabled him to attend Ranelagh School, Bracknell, the only Church Grammar School in the Diocese of Oxford. During the First World War, being under the minimum age acceptable for the Armed Forces, he volunteered for the Army having put his age up, but after three days' service his real age was detected and he was sent home. From 1920 until 1922 he attended the St. John's Training College, Battersea, London, passing the Board of Education's Final Examination for Students in Training Colleges in 1922 and became 'recognised by the Board' under the Code of Regulations for Public Elementary Schools as a Certified Teacher from 1st August 1922. Subjects included in the Student's Course of Study were 'The Principles and Practice of Teaching', Hygiene, Physical Training, English, History, Geography, Singing and Theory of Music and Drawing. He then took up teaching appointments at Bracknell Council School, Sunningdale Council School and St. Mary-in-the-Castle Senior School, Hastings, Sussex before taking the post of Headmaster at East Ilsley Council

School in January 1932. During his period at Hastings (2.11.1927 to January 1932) he was well thought of, being described as a capable teacher and a firm disciplinarian. He had a 'pleasant manner and his pupils were fond of him, but he was never familiar with them, in consequence of which he held their respect'. During 1930 the school won eight Open Championship Trophies for Football, Swimming and Athletic Sports – 'Mr Allen doing his share towards gaining them, for he always freely gave of his own time, out of school hours, for the benefit of his pupils'. Whilst at Hastings my father raised many thousands of pounds for the Royal British Legion and its associated charities, for which he was granted 'Membership for Life' of the Hastings Branch of the British Legion.

In December 1926 my father married my mother, Edith Marian TALBOT, also born in 1901, a native of Dunham-on-Trent, Near Newark, Nottinghamshire, the daughter of a Dairy Farmer. During the First World War my mother and her two sisters gave their services as V.A.D. Nurses, whilst her three brothers were serving in the Army in France, the youngest dying of his wounds in France in 1917. She later gained employment at the Broadmoor Criminal Lunatic Asylum and rose to the rank of Charge Attendant. On marriage she gave up her employment and did not work again until starting teaching (Needlework) in a part-time capacity at East Ilsley Council School during World War II. I was in fact born in Hastings in September 1931, arriving at East Ilsley at the age of four months.

On arriving at East Ilsley, the family took up immediate residence at the School House, East Ilsley, taking over Miss Rose Woodage as Maid from the previous occupants. Tom ALLEN settled down quickly, both at the school and to life in a village which was known throughout the United Kingdom for its involvement in Horse Racing and Sheep Rearing.

On 28th November and 12th December, 1934, East Ilsley Council School received a favourable report from Her Majesty's Inspector, Board of Education, a Mr. J.B. REYNISH. He drew attention to the very interesting last paragraph which read as follows: 'There is no Handicraft for the boys or Domestic Science for the girls, but last year the boys commenced to take Gardening on a suitable plot of ground adjacent to the playground. It is suggested that consideration be given to the inclusion in the Gardening Class of the older girls some of whom are exceptionally well grown and vigorous.'

Whilst on the subject of the 'School Garden', I would like to state that I well remember the splendour and lay-out of all the flowers being greatly admired by the whole village and worthy of very high praise by any judge during the mid-1930s. The school garden was enclosed on the West, South and East sides by a metal paling fence and on the North side by the Churchyard brick wall. The only 'blot on the landscape' was a plot of land of about ten square yards in the South-West corner where the contents of all the bucket lavatories situated on both the school premises and house were dug in by spade and buried. In 1939, in accordance with the 'Dig for Victory' campaign all the school garden and much of the house garden were turned over to the production of vegetables. A hole was also dug by the school children in the South part of the school garden where a small air-raid shelter was placed. Fortunately, it was never used.

Life in East Ilsley is well covered in Jim Wilson's 'East Ilsley – Photographic Memories 1900-1970' so I will only cover those activities I remember which were not included in the excellent publication.

I well remember listening to the wireless in the 'Living Room' of the School House to the Funeral of King George V, which left a lasting impression on me. I also remember going on a school outing to Harwell Aerodrome circa 1938 and waving a 'Union Jack' as King George VI and Queen Elizabeth drove along the old A34 into the main entrance. About the same period, I was standing in the area of the Living Room and Kitchen of the schoolhouse watching my mother cooking the 'Sunday Dinner' when a terrible thunderstorm erupted overhead and the Southern wall of the schoolhouse was struck by lightning and a thunderbolt landed near the Boys' School Playground. The strike resulted in a severe crack running from the roof to the foundations of the house, which was still visible when we left the village in 1948. Many of the electric plugs in the house were blown out of the sockets into the opposite walls, one in the Living Room missing me by inches. My father kept the thunderbolt on his school desk as a paper weight for many years. My mother was particularly apprehensive during the storm as one of her first cousins residing in Nottinghamshire had been struck whilst in his pram a few years previously, causing him to have a 'withered arm' for the rest of his life.

For the period 1932 to 1948 the whole of the school premises could be used as either one large room or divided into two rooms, one housing the Infants, and the other housing the Junior and Senior classes. The division was made possible by two movable metal partitions separated by a very windy passage with glass panelled doors at either end. In the event of these doors being opened at either end at the same time on a windy day, a North-South wind would rush through the passage in almost an uncontrollable manner and I do remember one pupil badly injuring his arm through his arm being forced through the glass panel of the door. The Senior and Junior classes in the large room were separated by a drawn curtain. This situation proved to be rather difficult when the Head Teacher and the Assistant Teacher were in full flow verbally.

During the period 1936 to 1938 I was taught by Marjorie Holmes and from 1938 to 1942 by Miss Hiscock and my father, the latter experience I would not wish on anyone. Calling my father 'Sir' during school activities both inside and outside the school and 'Dad' at home did not go down well, especially when my school misdemeanours were brought up again at home after school with painful results.

During my period in the Infants, I found Marjorie Holmes to be fairly strict but also very kind and thoughtful. Once a year she would invite all her pupils to her home in Down End, Chieveley, for a party which included wonderful refreshments and plenty of 'hide and seek' in her spacious garden. During this period all the Infants were very fortunate during playtimes in inclement weather in being able to enjoy many toys and a 'rocking horse' which had been generously donated by Harry and Mrs Graves who were Landlord and Landlady at The Crown Hotel at the time. The Infant Teacher at the school was usually the only pianist and therefore the school piano was normally kept in the Infants Room, being pushed into the other room on important occasions.

Before starting school I did have some insight into what life was like at school as I regularly 'played' in the schoolhouse garden which was adjacent to the school playgrounds, and even managed to disgrace myself on one occasion at the age of three. The Rector of the Parish at the time was one Arthur Ogle who was married to Mary with two children. The Rev. Ogle had graduated from Oxford and was a contemporary of George Bernard Shaw at Oxford, apparently getting into 'many scrapes' together. On occasions the Rector and his wife would consider it necessary to visit the schoolhouse without prior notice. On one such occasion the front doorbell went whilst my mother was in the midst of housework and my father was out. On hearing the doorbell, my mother exclaimed, "Oh it is the Rector again – I wonder if he has brought his bed this time?" The door was duly opened and the Rector and his wife formally welcomed. I then looked up at the Rector and said, "Have you brought your bed?" The Rev. Ogle, taken aback, answered, "What did that child say?"!

Having been successful at Hastings with athletics, my father endeavoured to continue the interest at East Ilsley and being a qualified AAA coach; he coached pupils up to and including 'County Level'. One very successful pupil was in fact Pam Arnold who achieved greatness at County level at an athletic meeting held at the Royal Military Academy, Sandhurst. My father, also being a qualified Berks and Bucks Football Referee, took great interest in the East Ilsley Football Club who played on a pitch just off the Abingdon Road. The pitch ran from North to South, but unfortunately had a slope from East to West which proved a problem for visiting teams.

During the years running up to World War II my father regularly organised coach outings to the International Military Tattoo at Aldershot which always took place in the evening. This event was well enjoyed by the participants but did cause the organiser some difficulties in getting everyone back to the coach at 2230 through a large crowd during the hours of darkness. The Reliance Bus Company, Chaddleworth (Proprietors – The Hedges family) was always used for school outings as their vehicles were considered more upmarket than the Newbury and District Bus Company and cost less.

The 'Horse Racing Industry' being one of the main employers in the area, it was natural that there was a great interest in it throughout the village by adults which left its mark on the children attending the school. Bets were illegally placed with the Landlords of the local public houses and were collected once a week by a Bookmaker from Southampton Street, Reading, known as 'Smiler Smith'. His visits to collect the bets and pay out the 'winnings' were eagerly awaited by the residents of the village, not only to receive their 'winnings' but to also enjoy his hospitality as he was in the habit of 'paying for drinks all round'.

A close liaison was always maintained between the 'Berkshire Constabulary' and the residents of the village. During the thirties we were fortunate in having a Police Station with cells, a Police House and a visiting Magistrates' Court from Wantage. The Police Station was occupied by Sergeant Charles Claydon and the Police House by Constable George Lynn. It is alleged that on one occasion the Reverend Ogle had cause to speak to PC Lynn regarding the performance of his duties in that he was not appearing in court as often as he should.

Some weeks later PC Lynn called at The Rectory and asked the Rev. Ogle to produce his 'Dog Licence'. The Rector was unable to produce a valid document and the Constable duly reported him for the offence, remarking that it was hoped that the Rector would now consider that he was performing his duties in a correct manner.

Police Officers were made welcome at the school and on one occasion I remember a Constable coming to talk on the subject of 'Protected Birds' Eggs' and the fact that it had come to notice that some had been stolen. As the Constable was speaking to the school, one small lad went as red as a beetroot indicating that he might well be guilty of such an offence. The Constable let the situation pass, but nevertheless made the point to all present that the theft of protected birds' eggs would not be tolerated. Talking of The Rectory and dogs, at one stage during my father's reign at East Ilsley, the Rector's son returned from South Africa and brought with him a large Alsatian dog which had to be placed in quarantine for six months. After its release my father was attending a 'Village Fete' in the grounds of The Rectory when the Alsatian knocked him over and grabbed my father's throat with its teeth. Whilst no serious injury was sustained, my father became petrified of all dogs for the rest of his life and often used a walking stick to fend off any unwelcome approach by such animals.

During the period 1932 to 1945, East Ilsley was well served by retailers namely C.J. Hibbert (Grocer and Baker), Bartholomew (General Store), Pickett (Confectionery), Warren Dudden (Butcher) and The Post Office (Postmistress Miss Eagles). Milk, bread, meat (by Dennis Dudden from Harwell) and newspapers were all delivered to the door and on Thursdays and Saturdays a 'Carrier' called to ascertain whether any residents would like him to make purchases for them in Newbury which would be delivered later the same day. We had a doctor (Dr Risien) resident in the village, who was 'on call' 24 hours a day. In 1935 I contracted 'double pneumonia' after the 'measles' and was very seriously ill. At the height of my illness, Dr Risien stayed by my bed all night until I was over the worst. I still claim today that he saved my life and I have always considered that I and my parents have been greatly indebted to him and his expertise. Both a nurse and a dentist (Miss Scanlon) regularly visited the school, the dentist carrying out any work on teeth necessary at a later date at Beedon Village Hall. We were also well served with buses between East Ilsley and Newbury, and East Ilsley and Reading, with buses to West Ilsley on Thursdays and Saturdays.

My paternal grandmother being resident in Crowthorne, Berkshire, the Allen family when visiting Crowthorne would travel via a Newbury and District single deck bus from East Ilsley to Thorn Street, Reading, walk from Thorn Street to the Railway Station and then catch a number three Thames Valley bus out to Crowthorne. On one occasion, during the early part of World War II, we had boarded the bus at East Ilsley which was rather crowded, complete with driver behind the partition, Charlie Bishop, and Bill Bradfield (a former pupil who commuted to school from Churn on foot) as conductor. We had covered about five miles and arrived at Ashampstead. Unfortunately, after the bus had stopped and picked up a couple of passengers, the conductor caught his hand in the back door of the bus and broke his finger. On witnessing the unfortunate occurrence, my father immediately took charge, instructing my mother to sit with the conductor on the long back seat of the bus and strap up the broken finger. My father then instructed the driver to deviate from his route and take the bus and passengers to the local doctor's surgery. The doctor duly treated the conductor but he was unable to continue with his duties. The conductor was returned to the back seat and my father, having removed the equipment from the conductor, adorned himself with money pouch, punch and ticket rack and proceeded to take the fares of any new passengers which frequently meant him calling out at the top of his voice, "Bill how much is it to Reading from so and so".

Whilst talking about N & D buses, the crews in those days usually spent most of their time in Public Houses at either end of their journeys, playing darts. If they were in the middle of a game of darts and the weather and road conditions were not too good, they would come to the conclusion that the bus could not travel on its next journey and get my father to ring Head Office in Newbury, where he was acquainted with the Managing Director, and get that particular journey cancelled. Also, because of his friendship with the MD, if travelling from East Ilsley to Newbury to catch a train from Newbury Railway Station, he would get the bus driver to divert his journey from the Wharf to drop the Allen family at the Railway Station.

Talking of the Allen family going on holiday, the day before embarking on such, my father would approach his senior pupils and ask them if anyone would be willing to transport the family luggage from the schoolhouse to 'The Square'. There was always an immediate positive response and a pupil, together with a truck made up of two pieces of wood and four pram wheels, would arrive at the appropriate time at the back door of the schoolhouse. There would then be a procession to the bus stop in 'The Square', the truck leading, my father immediately behind and my mother and myself taking up the rear two paces behind my father. En route to 'The Square', many village residents along the route would pass on their best wishes for a happy holiday.

During the period under review all 'school stock' (exercise books, blotting paper, foolscap paper, pens, nibs, slates and many other such items) would be despatched from the Berkshire Education Stores in Reading via the Great Western Railway to Compton Railway Station. On arrival at Compton, the Station Master would send a note to the school, neither the school nor the schoolhouse being on the telephone in those days. The Headmaster would then nominate four senior boys to take two 'trucks' to Compton to pick up the goods. Any pupil selected for this task greatly enjoyed the experience as they were told to 'take their time and not get involved in any incidents'. They did not have to cover the four-mile round trip within any specified time other than that they must be back at school before the end of the 'school day'. To my knowledge, no problem ever arose over this method of transportation, despite the boys not being under any form of supervision.

During my period at East Ilsley, few valuable toys were given to children which meant that we all had to amuse ourselves in what would be considered today a 'primitive manner'. Such amusements consisted of playing with cardboard boxes, snail racing, hopscotch in the road, building bicycles from old parts and then riding them – the only braking system consisting of placing your foot on the front mudguard, and bowling old tyres with a stick – the old tyres frequently going out of control and crashing through the gate of No. 1 Council House in to the well-kept vegetable garden of Geordie Russell, a local retired stable lad with an excellent vocabulary to fit. When none of these activities were convenient, there were always the elm trees just outside the East fence of the girls' school playground to climb. Many a meeting of juveniles took place seated near the top of these trees where matters of great international importance were discussed, especially after the outbreak of World War II.

As far as the school was concerned, outside activities continued throughout the period. Rounders was played in the 'Puzzle Field' and cricket was played to the West of the old A34 in a field just off a track which ran from East to West past Gilberts Racing Stables. Maurice Wilson, the well-known local farmer, kindly allowed a pitch to be constructed in this field which was regularly mown and rolled by the school children during the cricket season. On warm sunny days the Headmaster would despatch senior pupils in the school to various points of interest in the village and instruct them to record such buildings on paper with the aid of pencils and crayon. During the period the children were involved in the task, he would take a general stroll from one point of interest to another, commenting on their work and at the same taking in the marvellous fresh air that East Ilsley has always been famed for.

Circa 1937/1938, the dark clouds of possible war began to creep over the country and many local preparations were made should hostilities break out. The Berkshire Constabulary and Berkshire Special Constabulary appeared to take the lead in such matters. Later the Royal Observer Corps came under the jurisdiction of the Royal Air Force and was supervised by Commissioned Officers of the RAF. About the same time as the ROC was formed, volunteers were asked for, to form the 'Local Defence Volunteers' which later became the Home Guard. My father was a member of the LDV but not the Home Guard as he was fully employed with being the local Chief Observer in the ROC and his post as Headmaster. I well remember my father and others as members of the LDV dressed in denims and carrying broom handles, patrolling the Ridgeway with the instructions to look out for enemy parachutists. I also remember him dressed in his ROC uniform, which consisted of RAF-type serge tunic and trousers, a dark blue beret with a silver badge and a huge light blue greatcoat. I remember a few members, but by no means all, namely Harry Pearce (Sadler and Postman), Ernie Morby, Tom Allen, Mrs Rumble (who later emigrated to Australia with her husband and family), Mrs Edwards (wife of Group Captain Jumbo Edwards – later the coach of the Oxford University Boat Race Team living at The Mill, West Ilsley Road, which had an air strip just before and during the war), Redge Hurst (Landlord of The Swan), and then Warren Dudden (Butcher), Cyril Hibbert (Grocer and Baker). The Royal Observer Corps was responsible for picking out enemy aeroplanes in the sky, plotting their route and then reporting the sighting to the ROC HQ. All members of the ROC Post (which consisted of a dug-out and a portable shed above ground) were required to be fully proficient in recognising the type of enemy aircraft and firing .303 rifles. To become proficient in recognising the aircraft, they were issued with diagrams of the aircraft on cards in black and white, one aeroplane on each card. I well remember testing my father on recognition of enemy aircraft with the aid of these cards at least once a week. My father also had to prepare the times of duty for each member each week, covering 24 hours a day/seven days a week once the war had started. He had volunteered to join the British Army early in 1939 but had been turned down, mainly because of age. He was greatly disappointed but consoled himself that he had a school and Observer Corps post to run, which obviously took up all his time.

During the extensive bombing of Coventry, the ROC members reported that they could see the red glow in the sky caused by the bombing. A number of aircraft, both enemy and our own, crash-landed in the surrounding area and a few bombs aimed at Harwell and satellite aerodromes came down very near to the village. The first were 'oil bombs' which fell to the North of the village. Much later I well remember two 'high explosive bombs' screaming through the air which went into the ground without explosion less than a mile to the West of the school (about the middle of the present A34 Trunk Road). They were exploded the next day by 'Bomb Disposal' and left huge craters. Had they exploded on impact in the first place, neither the school nor the schoolhouse would be in existence today. The East Ilsley members of the ROC endeavoured to keep themselves well entertained during quiet periods by playing cards right through to more active pursuits such as shooting pheasants with the issued .303 rifles. On one occasion a Commissioned Officer of the Royal Air Force carrying out a spot inspection of the 'Post' was unable to ascertain why a number of rounds of .303 ammunition were missing.

During the period 1938/1939 and throughout World War II, my father endeavoured to maintain the interest of all pupils in the build up to war and the progress of the war. In order to do this, he would cut out all relevant maps etc out of daily newspapers and encourage the pupils to do the same and bring them to school. He would then place the maps on the blackboard and point out their importance answering questions along the way. A few days before the outbreak of World

War II there were massive BEF troop movements along the A34 in a Southerly direction and it was understood that the A34 was very heavily congested all the way from Birmingham to Southampton. Because of the heavy congestion, vehicles were often at a standstill with all the troops singing songs at the top of their voices, everyone being of the impression that the war would soon be over and that our troops would be returning victorious. During this period, I remember Staff Sergeant Bill Merrell coming home resplendent in his army uniform and later one of the Carter family coming home very proud in Royal Naval uniform and knocking on the back door of the school and thanking my father 'for making a man of him'. The same day I saw Carter seated high up in one of the elm trees outside the school playground surrounded by all his friends who were absolutely glued to his revelations (in complete silence) regarding his experiences in war at sea. Sadly he perished shortly afterwards when his ship was torpedoed and was never seen again. I remember Sidney Tindall being called up as a 'Bevan Boy' to serve in the coal mines, which must have been a nerve-wracking experience for both him and his family. Sadly, he was involved in a mining accident causing severe injuries to his head. Fortunately, he lived to tell the tale.

To many younger persons World War II started off as a great adventure and you often saw boys between the ages of about eight and 14 marching up and down the roads of East Ilsley in threes carrying sticks as rifles under the supervision of a 12-year-old 'Sergeant Major', namely Teddy Mills. Teddy Mills was also very popular as he was in the habit of inviting all his mates into his house at No.4 Council Houses to watch his 'Magic Lantern' show. Speaking of Ted reminds me of a very interesting true story regarding his, I believe, Grandfather

Edwin? Mills. Back in the 1930s, Edwin Mills believed he had reached retirement age but could not secure his old age pension as he had no birth certificate and could not prove his age accurately to the day. This caused him great consternation and he approached my father about the problem. After talking to my father for some time he happened to mention that he had received the cane at school for some offence. My father immediately went to the black-covered 'School Punishment' register and found that on a certain date whilst attending the 'Old School, Compton Road' an Edwin Mills at the age of eight had received six strokes of the cane. Having found this information my father quickly deducted Edwin's date of birth and informed the Ministry of Pensions. Edwin was granted a backdated Old Age Pension.

In August, 1939, my father and mother took me for a fortnight's holiday to Rottingdean, Near Brighton, the home of a famous comedian at the time, Max Miller. Two incidents occurred during that holiday, memories of which have always remained with me through the years, namely my father dressed up as a mother and pushing another male friend in a pram as a baby through the streets of Rottingdean on the occasion of the annual carnival. They were awarded the first prize of a silver-plated cigarette box each and later met up with Max Miller in what was then The White Horse Hotel. The second incident was more personal to me in that my parents took me into a 'Pet Shop' to choose a kitten. As we were travelling back by train, it was not convenient to bring the kitten home with us and alternative arrangements were made for the transfer of the kitten to East Ilsley. As World War II was being declared at 1100 hours on 3rd September 1939, the kitten arrived via a 'Carrier' at the Observer Corps Post at East Ilsley. I was standing there with my father at the time, not expecting such an event, but became very excited on noticing a tabby paw appear out of a window in a cardboard box. I immediately named the cat 'Mick' and I remained very close to him right through the war. He was run over by a car near The Puzzle on V E Day. In 1932 when my parents arrived at East Illsley, we had an 'Irish Terrier'. He was put down after being found consuming all Mr Gilbert's (Racehorse Trainer) guinea fowl. During the war my parents also took on another blue and black kitten, 'Winkle'. This cat used to meet my father whenever he returned to the house. One evening he was not in his usual place but later found drowned in the water butt outside the kitchen – apparently having got on to the lid which gave way, throwing the animal into the water. At East Ilsley we were more lucky with chickens than other pets!

One of the saddest memories I have of the beginning of World War II was the arrivals of evacuees from London at the time of the London Blitz. I remember two groups arriving at an interval of approximately three months. Both groups arrived at 'The Old School', East Ilsley, on a winter's evening during the hours of darkness. The first group came from the West Ham area of London and the second from Dagenham. Both groups were dealt with in the same unfortunate way in that they were placed on the stage of The Old School and the local East Ilsley residents selected whom they wished to take home. In the case of my parents, they took back to the schoolhouse the children who had not been selected, in each case this consisted of three boys. Although the evacuees came from poor circumstances, they had experienced in many cases water by the tap and flush toilets, although it must be admitted that many had not seen either a sheep or cow in the flesh before. At this time water at East Ilsley was either obtained from a well in the garden or in the majority of cases from one of the three manual water pumps (two situated in the Council House area near the school and one situated near the village pond) and then carried back to the house by yoke and buckets. In the case of the schoolhouse, water was brought up from the well in the garden and pumped across to the house. To have a bath in those days in the village was by way of a portable tin bath. At the schoolhouse there was a large bath standing on end in a kitchen cupboard which was lowered down into the kitchen when required for use, taking up the entire floor space. The back door had to remain ajar in order that the waste pipe could run from the bath to the drain outside. On bringing the three children home in each case my mother would bathe them in turn after removing all their clothing, which would later be washed in a large copper, heated by wood and coal, situated in a hut in the school playground. She would then make a set of trousers and a jerkin for each boy from old serge uniforms discarded by members of staff of the Broadmoor Criminal Lunatic Asylum. Having restored the boys to a state of cleanliness, she would then ensure that they were well fed and allocated the third bedroom which was sparsely furnished. As far as schooling was concerned, all village children attended school in the morning and all the evacuees attended in the afternoon. At first there were disciplinary problems, but they were quickly laid to rest and the system worked reasonably well under the circumstances. There was, however, a massive culture problem and in both cases many of the children returned back to their homes in London despite the blitz, their parents not being happy with what they witnessed on visiting their children in East Ilsley. In fairness some of the children were very happy with their new-found homes and remained in East Ilsley indefinitely becoming 'pillars of society'.

A SUMMARY OF FURTHER MEMORIES OF
THE WORLD WAR II YEARS 1939 TO 1945

1. Miss Gilbert took over the Infants Department, cycling to and from her home in London Road, Newbury in all weathers.

2. The Puzzle farm buildings opposite the school were badly damaged by fire on two occasions.

3. A number of fundraising auctions took place in the Old School, Compton Road on such occasions as 'Wings for Victory Week'. My father, accompanied by pupils and their trucks, would tour the village requesting items for auction. He would then conduct the auction (letting no person with money escape) but in actual fact any purchaser was investing their money as an equivalent number of National Savings stamps would be issued in return for the cash. As a result of these auctions many thousand of pounds' worth of National Savings stamps were sold which obviously benefited the country.

4. A touring cinema visited the Old School on occasions showing such films as George Formby in 'The Sky's the Limit'. These performances were well attended.

5. Dancing to 'Live Bands', 'Whist Drives', and amateur dramatic performances by members of the Women's Institute frequently took place in the Old School.

6. Rabbits, hares, pheasants etc were frequently thrown over garden fences on the instructions of local farmers after a shoot.

7. Many residents in the village kept chickens in their gardens providing a regular supply of fresh eggs.

8. Celebrities such as Flanagan and Allen (Comedians), Freddy Mills (Boxer) and Terry Ashwood (Middle East War Correspondent at the time but normally a Director of Pathe Gazette Newsreels) visited the village.

9. The Piano in The Sun Public House, usually played by Joan White, provided a regular Saturday night sing-a-long.

10. Circa 1942 bad snowstorms hit the village and the surrounding countryside, causing very deep drifts which tended to swallow whole vehicles. Cyril Hibbert was caught in one of these blizzards and he and his van were nearly buried alive. The whole working population being unable to carry out their normal tasks would turn out en bloc with shovels to restore 'normality'. The village was sometimes cut off for many days on end. Despite the many problems caused by the weather the school never admitted defeat and closed – lessons being carried out in the usual manner. If the weather was very bad, pupils were allowed to go home a little earlier than usual. It was not unusual for me and my fellow pupils to have to walk home from Newbury, the weather having deteriorated since arrival at school to such an extent to stop all transport home.

11. Owing to shortage of manpower in the village my father
frequently assisted Messrs Eacott and Gregory Undertakers (also
Builders, Painters & Decorators) to carry coffins at funerals.

MEMORIES OF THE SCHOOLHOUSE, EAST ILSLEY

Prior to World War II

The house had been built quite recently and was considered very modem by standards in the village at the time. Although it was connected to electricity, there were no gas, mains water, sewerage or drainage.

The ground floor consisted of a 'Front Room', 'Living Room', Kitchen and a Hall. The 'Front Room' was situated to the West of the Hall and was a very pleasant room receiving the sun from midday onwards. There were windows facing the South and West and in the room was a built-in glass-front cupboard. Heating was by way of a coal fire. The room was furnished with a three-piece suite and table, but was only used to entertain visitors and when the 'Living Room' chimney was being cleaned. The 'Living Room' was on the East side and adjacent to the staircase. This room was used for all meals and most of the day was in fact spent in the room. The room was furnished with an antique mourning table, two high carved back antique chairs and two similar dining chairs. There was a very large dresser in the room as a permanent fixture. The only entertainment consisted of an old wireless set which operated on accumulators which were charged by C.J. Hibbert, Grocers. The only furniture in the kitchen was an old scrubbed table. Heating and cooking in the kitchen was by way of an old range to which black lead was applied daily. An old deep kitchen sink was used for personal hygiene, washing up etc. Next to the sink was a hand pump which was used twice a week to pump water from the well-house to the tank in the attic. Immediately outside the kitchen door was a 'coursey' (i.e. a hard standing) surrounded by an eight foot high wooden fence. Off the coursey was situated a coal shed immediately on the right of the back door and to the right round a corner was a large 'bucket' toilet. In those days in East Ilsley, toilet soap and toilet rolls were virtually unheard of. Sunday newspapers were cut up into small strips and large bars of a primitive tar soap were in daily use.

The first floor consisted of a landing on the South side with a window overlooking Asbridge Hill. The main bedroom was to the West and my old bedroom to the East with windows looking towards the West and East respectively. The third smaller room was between the two with a window looking North. Heating was by way of coal fires.

The Hall was rather spacious and the front door a 'rather grand affair'. Much of the hall was taken up with the protrusion of the bath cupboard from the kitchen. In the gap between the rear of the cupboard and the 'Front Room' was a very large high back armchair which was very old.

The garden was spacious and very well laid out. There were three well-kept lawns, numerous flower beds and an orchard consisting of apple and plum trees.

Many interesting shrubs were present and the area below the 'Living Room' was a well-kept vegetable garden. On the North side of the house, a large fitted dog kennel had been built adjacent to the wall.

During and after World War II

Apart from the main lawn on which was situated the large walnut tree, all other lawns and similar areas were all dug up in order to cultivate vegetables. Paths remained intact and some flower beds and shrubs were retained. The whole garden was surrounded by a metal paling fence with metal gates. Throughout my time in the house, no one appeared to ever oil the front gate, possibly so that my father and mother were made aware whenever it was entered.

I successfully passed the 'entrance examination' to St. Bartholomew's Grammar School, Enborne Road, Newbury and commenced my education there in September 1942 (halfway through World War II).

St. Barts was first founded in 1466 and until the Education Act of 1944 was a 'Private Fee-paying School'. My parents were required to pay fees each term and for 'Bus Season Ticket', all 'TextBooks', all 'Exercise Books', one for each subject (a different coloured cover for each), and all sports clothing, together with 'Rugby Football boots', plimsoles and School Dinners. On top of all this expense, a school uniform consisting of black jacket with either black pin striped trousers or grey flannels for two terms and a green blazer with the school badge thereon for the summer term. A school cap and tie, white shirts and black shoes.

School consisted of five full days from 0845 until 1530 hours Monday to Friday and normal school periods from 0845 until 1230 on Saturdays. On Saturday afternoons you were expected to attend school sports. From the third form upwards you were required to join either the Army Cadet Force, Air Training Corps or Sea Cadet Corps (and attend 'Summer Camps'.) On Mondays you went to school in 'Military Uniform' (supplied by the school) for compulsory 'Military Training' on Monday afternoons. Sport was played on Wednesday afternoons, which consisted of rugby in the winter and cricket and athletics in the summer term.

School Rules were onerous and applied during term time only:

1. If when you arrived at school you were not in full school uniform you were sent home (no matter what distance was involved) to rectify the situation.

2. Boys should wear their school caps from the time of leaving home until return.

3. No boys were allowed to enter F.W. Woolworth Stores or any 'slot machine arcades' during term time.

4. No boys were allowed to attend or play in Association Football Games during term times, particularly Reading Football Club.

5. To be on best behaviour at all times when travelling on 'Public Transport'.

The responsibility for enforcement of these rules both on school premises and outside was left with the School Prefects (about 20 in number) who duly issued 'Yellow Report Cards' to offenders. The 'Report Cards' covered one week and should they be marked N.S. at any time during the week the offender would be required to report to the Prefects Room (situated in one of the towers protruding from the school roof) for punishment administered by one Prefect in the presence of all Prefects. Punishment consisted of being struck on the buttocks with the sole of a size 12 plimsole on a number of occasions depending on the offence involved. (I fell foul of this situation on a number of occasions whilst at the school for trivial offences. On one occasion I was found to have secreted a comic in my pants. Result: struck with pants removed – a very sore experience.)

St. Barts was well blessed with sports facilities and besides the area at the back of the school also two other sports fields, one in Enborne Road and another across Fifth Road (Fifth Road running adjacent to the school field) with a Pavilion. One of the boundaries (a wooden fence) to the Fifth Road field also formed the boundary to the County School for Girls catering for the 11 to 18 age group. In 1944 St. Barts became a 'State Funded School' and later circa 1970s became a Comprehensive School for Boys, which resulted in the two schools amalgamating. Much later the St. Barts original buildings were either demolished or converted into flats and a new school was built in the Fifth Road sports field. At a reunion for all boys and girls who attended the original schools during the Second World War, the Headmaster at the time of the reunion during an address of welcome made great play on the relationship which must have been formed between the girls and boys during that period, making the comment 'that the only contraceptive facility available at the time was in fact a wooden fence'.

As a result of the Education Act of 1944, my parents were no longer required to pay fees and the season travelling ticket was paid for by the state.

Morning Assembly started at 0845 hours with a 'Piano Recital of Classical Music' by the' Art and Music Master', but those travelling in from the country villages by train or bus could not make this time and waited in the hall until completion when they were admitted. A hymn and prayers conducted by the Headmaster followed, after which there was a further opportunity of pupils to enter the main hall. Pupils were expected to travel to school in all weathers and throughout my six years at the school I never experienced the school closed for any reason including air raids, extreme snow conditions etcetera, despite the central heating situation being in very bad condition. If the heating was down you put on your outer clothes and ran around the sports field close to the hedges between periods. If the air raid siren went you left your classroom and ran along the same route under the hedges. On many occasions the buses stopped running in bad weather and in my case I had to walk the 11 miles home with other pupils. We never complained, our parents were never unduly concerned, and we even enjoyed the experience to some extent.

Until I went to Grammar School, I led a very protected life at home. I was seldom allowed to leave the grounds of the house or school on my own, and I could only play with children who were invited to the house by my mother who was a very strict disciplinarian and very handy with both her hand and a copper stick. The consequence of this experience was that when I commenced Grammar School my whole lifestyle was changed to a very great extent and being a very shy, introverted child, I found this very difficult and I must say that I received no help whatsoever from either my mother or father – it was just a case 'of get on with it'.

The first day at a new school came along and I got out of bed at 0615, went down to the kitchen and washed myself at the kitchen sink. There was no bathroom room and no shower – the bath (stored in a cupboard in the kitchen) was only available once a week. Breakfast followed and at 0740 I left the house all dressed in my new school uniform together with a brand new, very large leather school satchel. Down the garden path, through the girls and boys' playgrounds, out on to the road adjacent to 29 Council Houses, down the hill, past the church, round by the pond and into the Square. Two buses, owned by the Newbury and District Bus Company, namely an old 1920s Leyland 32-seater and a new utility 32-seater with wooden slat seats (very restricted for room), were kept in a large garage at the back of The Swan Public House. The former was used for the first trip of the day to Newbury and then on to the Reading route from 1000 hours, and the latter solely on the Newbury route. The driver arrived on his bicycle and the Leyland brought out from the garage to The Square and off we went at 0800, arriving at The Wharf, Newbury at 0840 hours. En route we picked up about six Grammar School boys (none on their first day) and a School Prefect got on at Chieveley. We then walked to school via The Market Place, Bartholomew Street and eventually the Enborne Road. After assembly (or the last part of it) I was conducted to my new 1a Classroom on the ground floor where we were all greeted by Mr Littleberry, our

31

Form Master, who proved to be an absolute gentleman –retired but had been recalled in to his old role as many masters from the school were serving in HM Forces. The classroom was very old with a seat and desk for each pupil, full of engraved initials of past pupils, forming one unit. The windows were large but so high up on the wall that it was impossible to see out of them. Both the teacher's desk and blackboard were massive. Being anxious to prove popular with other pupils in the class, one of my early misdemeanours was aimed at upsetting our very excitable Austrian Teacher, 'Minsky', who had served in the First World War. I had secreted into school a morse code buzzer complete with wire etc, and placed one end in my desk and the other end in the Master's desk. I then started tapping out morse from my desk. On hearing the strange noise in his desk, Minsky started leaping about the classroom shouting "Where is that mouse" in Austrian, much to the laughter of the rest of the class. I got away with it – Minsky never knew the culprit.

The home journey consisted of walking from the school back to The Wharf to catch the 1610 hours bus getting off at the 'Top of the Hill', which was only one meadow away from the schoolhouse, entering the schoolhouse via the front gate, straight into the garden, this time just after 1700 hours; tea was usually ready. From Monday to Fridays during term time I only saw my father between the time I got home and the time he went off to the 'Pub' at 1820 hours. I brought this matter up with my mother on one occasion to which she replied abruptly, "Your father is dealing with children all day in school and it is necessary for him to get away to other company from that." I have often wondered throughout my life why that retort was necessary. Throughout my time at Grammar School my father only visited the school once, with my mother, when I was in the fourth form – more about that later. He never gave me any support of any kind or seemed to take any interest in my studies.

My mother's education consisted of a village school, leaving at 13 years of age. She endeavoured to take an interest, but this was of no use because the subjects dealt with were beyond her capabilities and her interruptions during 'Home Work' proved to be a great hindrance. My mother, however, did attend the 'School Play' and 'Speech Day' every year, but I was never informed of any contact with my teachers.

During the period of my upbringing the subject of 'Sexual Matters' was never discussed at home, within schools etcetera. I did, however, work with both sheep and cows for local farmers during my school holidays from the age of 11 and came into contact with 'Italian Prisoners' working on the farms which assisted in my sex education and of course the evacuees from London were helpful in this respect. I was never able to speak to my parents on the subject and to be quite honest would have been scared stiff even to approach to bring up the subject with them. I must state that at the age of about 14 I was raped by a youth of about 17 (I still vividly remember his name and address in the village). It was about midday in full view, whilst I was walking through a farmyard. He just rushed forward towards me without any comment, knocked me down and assaulted me. I managed to resist during the episode and give him a good belting with my foot in his nether regions. I was too scared to tell anyone of the incident, but I did notice that when I became a Police Cadet at Newbury shortly afterwards, both he and his family left the village for an unknown destination overnight.

All went well at St. Barts for about three years, during which I received good 'End of Term Reports' and managed to remain in the top half of the form as far as results were concerned. I managed to keep up with sports and the gymnasium and was reasonably happy. On Sundays I was involved in both Campanology and Choir twice a day at the local church, and on the summer evenings went for a walk to The Ridgeway in the evening. Towards the end of the 'School Year', however, things changed dramatically. I was sitting at my desk during a mathematics period, when the Deputy Headmaster (taking the subject) endeavoured to squeeze in beside me on my seat. He then placed his right arm around me and snuggled up to me, asking if I was getting on alright. My immediate reaction was to forcibly move his arm with a sharp downward action, which must have hurt him. This did not make him happy and for the remainder of my time at the school he constantly made my life a misery and on several occasions served me with a 'Report Card', always for 'Insolence'. On one occasion I had been to see the Headmaster over a matter and was late for the Deputy Headmaster's period. I knocked on the door and he shouted 'enter'. When I entered, in front of the whole class he served me with a Report Card for 'Insolence' for not knocking on the door. This attitude by the Deputy Headmaster continued but I did not mention it to my parents for fear of reprisals as they would always take the side of the Teacher.

Towards the end of the fourth year, parents were invited to a 'Parents Day' at the school on a Saturday afternoon, during which I visited the Forum Cinema in Newbury. During the afternoon my parents were seen by the Deputy Headmaster and told that I was one of the worst pupils they had in the school, being lazy and constantly insolent. My parents and I were due to travel home on the same double decker bus from the Wharf. When I arrived at the bus I found my parents sitting on a back seat of the bus facing the back entrance. As I got on, they turned their backs on me. I could see trouble was about, so decided to travel upstairs. Not a word was spoken until we got home when 'all hell took place' and all my so-called privileges were cancelled for three months. To say the least, life was even more difficult at home than usual for a very long period. I personally carried on working hard until sitting my Oxford and Cambridge School Certificate in the spring of 1947. I failed, but on taking it the following December I passed well.

In January, 1948 I returned to school to study 'Classics' in the Lower Sixth but in February on a very miserable day as far as weather was concerned I was approached by the Deputy Headmaster whilst studying in the School Library with the comment, "One of us is leaving this school, Allen, and I have no intention of leaving". He then left me. I waited until the morning break, put on my overcoat, walked to Newbury Police Station in Pelican Lane (a distance of two miles) and knocked on the closed front door. The door was opened and the Station Sergeant, Sergeant Walter Nicholls, asked me what I wanted. I said, "Have you got a job for me as a 'Boy Clerk'?" He said, "I see you are from St. Barts. We have had boys from there before. Yes, you can start on Monday morning at 0600. Shift work five days a week alternating between 0600 and 1400 and 1400 to 2200 at a wage of £1 per week." On the following Monday I got up at 0400 and started my journey on my bicycle at 0500 in poor weather conditions. I cycled the nine miles and reported on time where two middle-aged lady civilian clerks instructed me in my duties from 0900. At 1400 hours Constables Ray HUNT and Horace CADE of the Mobile Department took me home in an open Sunbeam Talbot Tourer patrol car with the cycle tied to the back. I will never forget their kindness and to this date I am still in touch with the Hunt family and reminding them of the kindness of their ancestors. For some reason I will never understand why my parents never questioned me about my actions and seemed reasonably happy at that time with my situation.

In May 1948 I was appointed one of the first Cadets in Berkshire with the collar number 10. During my first week as a Civilian Clerk, I was asked by the Switchboard Operator, a rather attractive lady of about 25 years who was applying her make-up in the Switch Board Room, to take an incoming call whilst she completed her task in hand. Having been asked before and getting rather tired of the request, I refused to act as suggested. She reported me to the Superintendent. I was duly called into his office and he said, "You have only been here four days and already have managed to upset the female staff. I have also heard that you are not careful when using the carbon paper thus rendering it unusable." After a few stern words he burst out laughing and said, "Never mind, you will learn. Go up the street and get me 20 Senior Service cigarettes."

Whilst at Newbury I was instructed to teach myself to use a typewriter. This I tried to do in a painful way. A Sergeant, Fred Costar, whom I had previously met in East Ilsley, a huge brute of a man, used to hit me on my left hand with an antique ebony ruler when not using both hands. After a time, however, I became quite proficient on the old three bank 'Oliver' which held me in very good stead for years to come, both in the Police Service and Army.

Although travelling between East Ilsley and Newbury in all weathers on shift work proved very onerous, my time at Newbury Police Station was reasonably happy. Unfortunately, that contentment came to an end at about 1500 hours on a weekday in August 1948.

On arriving home I found my mother in a state of distress (until this time I had always found her to be a very 'hard' woman) and between the tears she said, "I have to tell you that in ten days' time we are moving house to Wiltshire as your father has got another 'Headship' at a small village, namely Yatton Keynell."

I immediately replied, "What is going to happen to me and my job?"

She replied, "You will have to come with us and get a job on a farm or something when you get there."

Two days later I was dragged off with my parents via bus to Newbury, bus to Swindon, train to Chippenham and taxi to Yatton Keynell to view their new abode. Facilities were to say the least nowhere up to the standard of their present accommodation The house was attached to the school and the whole building was about 110 years old. Our bucket toilet was across the yard and the whole house was damp and dingy.

I learned later that many residents in the village had never been on a train or to the sea and many took their annual holidays a couple of miles away with friends and then sent holiday postcards back to their friends in Yatton Keynell. I just stood in the middle of the road in the heat of the summer sun absolutely devastated. I immediately protested to my parents: "No way am I coming to this dump". We returned to East Ilsley and after a few days I had managed to get a 'Compassionate Transfer' to Wokingham thanks to my Superintendent and a Chief Inspector, who had been stationed at Newbury, getting the post of Superintendent at Wokingham. My mother's sister, Aunty May, who had been widowed many years and left with no children, on hearing of the problem, offered me the third bedroom in her house at Crowthorne (very small but next to the only bathroom) on condition that when on early turn I assisted with the cleaning and when on late turn with the cooking. Her second bedroom was rented out to two sisters. Fortunately I got on well with my aunt and one of the sisters, but found the other, a Deputy Matron in a Mental Hospital, the same hospital where my aunt worked as a Sister, could be difficult at times.

On a Saturday in August 1948 an old Armstrong Siddeley Taxi arrived from Crowthorne driven by Ticker Lovick, an old friend of my father. After lunch the car was loaded with my few belongings and my Raleigh Bicycle was strapped on the back. During the 30-mile journey my mind was trying to solve many questions as to why I was in this situation, how much guidance and interest I had received from my parents during my life so far, what did the future hold for me, and above all why did my mother allow my weight to reach over 20 stone by force feeding me with 'Bubble and squeak' every night just before going to bed. I was shortly to find out that my mother's sister was to save the day for me in many, many ways. My father's family never proved particularly helpful in any way. (I had only seen my maternal grandparents three times before their death in1944.)

A couple of days later I visited another house in Crowthorne occupied by my grandmother, her single daughter and her single son. All three were at home and noted the fact that I was now lodging with Mother's sister, who they believed to be 'well off financially'. My grandmother said to me, "Your aunt is well able to look after you, but if you wish at any time you can come here for breakfast or dinner (in those days lunch was referred to as dinner), the charge for breakfast will be one shilling and dinner one shilling and sixpence). I left the house bemused.

On my first Monday at Wokingham I was required to report at 0900 for 0900-1700 duties. After that the shifts were 0700 to 1500 one week with 0900-1200 on Saturdays, and 1500 to 2200 the other week, with 1400 to 1700 on Saturdays. I spent my first day with Cadet Garth Borland, a very helpful chap living in Winnersh. At 0905, however, I took a telephone call from a lady who had found a 'Racing Pigeon' in distress and turned to Garth asking for details of disposal. At that minute Sergeant 'Rasher' Haines' Divisional Clerk Sergeant appeared on the scene and started giving a rollicking for not knowing the procedure. I answered back abruptly to the effect that I had only been at Wokingham Police Station for five minutes. He ignored the comment and stamped out of the telephone room, swinging his left arm in a characteristic manner. This was to be the first of my many 'run ins' with 'Rasher' over many years in the future. Little did I realise then Rasher would be my Shift Sergeant at Ascot and later my Inspector at Wallingford. Apart from Rasher, I found the whole staff at Wokingham very helpful and understanding. At 1250 that day the General Office staff upstairs adjourned for lunch and I quickly noticed a very attractive and well-groomed sixteen-year-old girl heading for the back door. I later ascertained from Garth that her name was Gwen and that she lived in Barkham Road, Wokingham and walked to and from her home for work. Apart from entering and leaving the station by the back door, we seldom saw Gwen downstairs and during my whole time at Wokingham I never got past 'Hello' with the girl until one morning towards the end of my time at Wokingham, we passed on the middle of the centre steep staircase when our eyes locked together for a brief minute. She was dressed in a nice green pullover, brown skirt and court shoes. Looking back, I think that was the start of our relationship, but being away for National Service for two years prevented any follow up.

During my time at Wokingham, I always cycled to and from work, a distance of four miles from Crowthorne. When on late shift I sometimes went to the Crowthorne Social Club for a game of snooker with David Bennett, the Steward, who literally befriended me. Some years later David's son became a Police Cadet at Bracknell and a Sergeant on Traffic Division of Thames Valley Police.

When I was on early turn, I went occasionally to the Plaza Cinema in Crowthorne (until it was burnt to the ground – arson always suspected) in the evening and on Saturday evenings I occasionally managed to get as far as the Majestic Ballroom in Reading but the two-mile walk home from the Crowthorne Railway Station at 2330 hours was a deterrent, especially during the winter in bad weather. Apart from David Bennett, I made very few friends outside the work place and certainly no girlfriends. On occasions my father did send me the train fare to Chippenham which enabled me to visit my parents from 1600 on a Saturday until 1500 on a Sunday. I always found the journey and visit very difficult, particularly during the winter.

My Aunt May was always very supportive but there was one occasion on a Saturday afternoon when her tolerance of my presence was put to the limit. She had flowerbeds in front of her detached house and a large vegetable garden and orchard at the rear, which she cared for herself. On this particular occasion I was helping her in the vegetable garden when she asked me to fetch one of her two antique wheelbarrows from her large shed. Without thinking, I picked up the wheelbarrow, not noticing that she had antique crockery stored on a piece of wood which covered the top of the barrow. Crash! All her antique crockery was smashed in an instant, causing her vocabulary to be extremely blue – not particularly surprising as she had worked among patients at the Broadmoor Criminal Lunatic Asylum for many years. I quickly got dressed and retired to the Majestic Ballroom at Reading. On my return to her house, 'Delamere', at about 0030 hours she came into my bedroom and apologised.

During my period of residence at Crowthorne, a local butcher, Charles Swain, unfortunately sold an amount of 'corn beef' which was contaminated and led to 32 local residents going down with 'Typhoid', two of whom tragically proved fatal. Very strong living constraints were enforced throughout the area. Despite my aunt being very considerate at all times, my life at Crowthorne proved to be very lonely outside the work situation and I certainly was not entirely unhappy when I was called up for National Service in January 1950. I received a 'Railway Warrant' for the journey from Crowthorne to Salisbury, together with instructions that I was to wear old clothing throughout which would be returned to my registered home address at Yatton Keynell shortly after my eventual arrival at Bulford Camp. I got out of bed at 0500 hours, walked to Crowthorne Railway Station on a very dark and cold morning, and boarded a train to Guildford where I had to change for Salisbury. The journey to Guildford proved to be very quiet, but on arrival at Guildford I found the platform for the Salisbury train heavily crowded with many National Service recruits also bound for Bulford. When we boarded the full train, everyone started to meet one another and sing. It all appeared to be very joyful but little did we know at that stage that many on board would be later killed in the lnjin River Battle in Korea, having been moved into the Gloucestershire Regiment. On arrival at Salisbury we were met by a very affable Sergeant Major who gave us a very warm welcome. Troop Carrying Vehicles were all awaiting our presence outside the station with steps supplied to climb into the rear of the vehicle. Off we went, still singing. On arrival at Bulford, everything suddenly changed to reality. The CSM regained his normal military self and there were no steps down from the trucks. In language I cannot repeat, we were ordered out of the vehicle in double quick time.

Within a short period we were stripped of all our clothing but allowed to retain our shoes, then followed army issue right down to socks, underwear, denims, uniform, great coat etc. We were issued with string and brown paper, told to make a parcel of all our civilian clothes and then marched to the Station Post Office where the parcel was despatched to your home address. The Quartermaster quickly found a problem with me as I was 6ft 5ins in height and overweight, and there were no uniforms or boots to fit me in the Stores. Two pairs of United States Army boots (without toe caps) and a steel helmet were issued to me, and they remained with me for the rest of my service. This situation of course invited questions from every 'Inspecting Officer' I came across throughout my service. Fortunately, two tunics and two pairs of trousers were tailored for me and issued three weeks later.

Later in the day we all received one type of haircut 'short, back and sides'. The more the chaps complained, the shorter the haircut. The haircuts were so bad that rumour had it that they were being carried out by non-skilled fatigue personnel.

As Barrack Rooms went in the Army at the time, they were quite reasonable at Bulford, and the food was not too bad. We were, however, required to 'double' everywhere and very much subject to 'Bugle Calls'. We were immediately subject to strict 'Infantry Training', but I quickly ascertained because I had obtained an Oxford and Cambridge Joint Board School Certificate together with my previous achievements in the Army Cadet Force whist at Grammar School, I was excused all 'Education Classes' and also elementary drill movements and elementary shooting training.

My previous achievements also excused me from all but the final interview with the War Office Selection Board for a Commission. As I had no desire to obtain a Commission and certainly no financial backing behind me to deal with Mess Bills etc, I declined the offer. I very soon realised that I had made the right decision mainly because the life of a National Service Second Lieutenant was not exactly a popular one.

Despite weight problems I managed to keep up with the very strict physical routine and bond a happy situation with my fellow soldiers.

After about four or five weeks, I and another ex Police Cadet from Gloucestershire, namely Ken HUDMAN, were ordered to report to the Company Sergeant Major after the usual morning parade. On arrival we were informed by the CSM we had been transferred to the RMP and posted to lnkerman Barracks, Woking for 16 weeks training that day and a 15cwt vehicle would pick us up at 1300 hours and take us to Salisbury Railway Station en route for Woking. We both protested that despite having been Police Cadets we had no wish whatsoever to join the RMP and at that stage had no intention of returning to the Civilian Police Force. Our protests were of no interest to him and were of no avail. The truck picked us up as arranged and we caught the train to Woking.

PLEASE NOW READ A PAPER BY JOLHN REDMAN which gives an excellent description of his life at lnkerman which proved to be identical in many ways to life at lnkerman.

MEMORIES OF INKERMAN
BARRACKS, WOKING, SURREY

By John Redman

Ah, Inkerman Barracks! What memories that name will invoke personnel who joined RMP prior to 1964. The place was opened as a Prison in 1860, and housed 300 male convicts. By 1870, using male prisoners as a labour force, the place had doubled in size, and contained 1,700 convicts, half of them being female. In 1889, the Home Office handed the site over to the War Office, and it was named Inkerman Barracks. It remained a military establishment until 1965, but more importantly for us, it was the home of the Corps of Royal Military Police from 1947 until 1964. I first saw the place in January 1958 when I arrived as a Voluntary Transfer from the Infantry. I had arrived at Woking Railway Station from Exeter, and a kindly Southern Railways employee told me that the next bus would take me to the main gate of the Barracks. I struggled on to the bus with great difficulty, carrying, as I was, all my military equipment, and I mean ALL, as I was wearing Field Service Marching Order [FSMO]. This comprised of Large Pack, Small Pack, Kitbag, which contained every item of military and civvy equipment I owned. Cross Straps, Basic Pouches, Waist Belt, all in 1937 pattern, and blancoed with Proberts Number 93, with brasses gleaming; a steel helmet and a big greatcoat made up the rest. Suitcases, soldiers for the use of, were unheard of then. What I didn't know, was that the bus I was on stopped in the village of St John's, and didn't go anywhere near the Barracks. So, I had to walk (struggle) up that long, steep hill to the village of Knaphill, and the main entrance to lnkerman. I walked past the Officer's Mess and single Officers accommodation on my left, with that superb sports field on my right. From the outset I could see that grim forbidding Main Block, and Clock Tower, ahead of me, standing high above all else. It certainly didn't get any prettier as I got closer either. Arriving at the Main Gate, I was unlucky enough to be met by the Provost Sgt, who decided to "crawl" all over me in some a form of ritualistic welcome. After handing in my Travel Documents, I was taken by a young soldier of the RAOC, who was awaiting RTU back to Blackdown, to the Main Block, and shown into an enormous empty barrack room on the second floor. The block was alive with blokes in various stages of training, and the noise of their studded boots echoed all around the stone walls and floors. I drew bedding, made my bed up and went back to the Guardroom for further instructions. I was sent to A Company offices (immediately on the right, opposite the Guardroom and inside the Main gate. B Company was on the other side, behind the Guardroom). A Sgt told me to piss off and get tea, and to report to the Company offices at 0730 the following morning. Thus started my 16 weeks of training at lnkerman. I didn't stay in that huge, empty cavern of a room in the Main Block for too long, before being sent to a squad forming up in the wooden Spiders at the rear of the camp. Now these Spiders I was used to from previous postings, and they were pure luxury compared to the Main Block. Even so, the Spiders would be considered to be positively antique and unhygienic to modem soldiers. We had to scrub the bare wooden floorboards every morning, and then had to leave the windows open all day long – remember it was winter too. The pot bellied metal stove (polished to a brilliant, gleaming black monument every morning) soon consumed the coal ration, and we froze unless we could "find" extra coal or coke. I seem to remember that the single officers' blocks were always good for a few lumps. Bed blocks had to be made every day, the blankets and sheets immaculately squared off and symmetrical, the bottom blanket pulled tight over the mattress and bed frame so that a penny coin could be bounced on it. Top Kit, comprising of both large, and small packs, together with all assorted straps, all polished brasses facing forward, was lined up all squared off and symmetrical on the tops of personal steel lockers. We slept on the floor before a big kit inspection so that we could lay out our gear the night before. There was always a mad rush to get to the washbasins, toilets and baths, as there weren't enough of them for the number of men in situ. The cookhouse served terrible grub, and we marched there from the Billets carrying our china mugs and "eating irons" clasped behind our backs in the left hand. The cooks who always gave you the hardest time were the RMP LCpls who had been trained as Regimental Cooks. After the "Meal" it was "scrape, wash and then rinse" your eating irons in the cold, stinking, greasy, fat covered water in the containers by the exit. Remember how your knife, fork and spoon finished up covered in white, oily fat? Do you guys remember the NAAFI where you could buy meat pies and chips, or sausage and chips, and have a decent cup of tea? We listened to Perry Como singing "Magic Moments" over and over again on the jukebox. Then there was the NAAFI shop in the little square between the Guardroom and the flagpole where we bought new leather bootlaces, blanco, Brasso, whitening, black Kiwi polish for bulling boots, and dark brown Kiwi polish for bulling chinstraps. The NAAFI assistant was called Lionel, who we referred to as a "Nancy Boy" as Gay meant something totally different then. If you annoyed Lionel, he would grab a bunch of leather bootlaces and give you a smack across the arm with them. Ammo boots were sent away to a Prison somewhere for repair, and if the Lags knew they were from the RMP, they would come back with the toes and heels slashed with a knife. The Kit inspections usually meant that if you were in the Main Block your kit was thrown out of the windows to come hurtling down onto the edge of the Square, or if you were in the Spiders, it was chucked into the smelly, green scummed water that filled the air raid shelters that were located between each building. (These were only blocked up in 1961 when I was at Inkerman as an Instructor.) How many times did you have to buy a new china mug – which you'd probably only bought the day before – because it was deemed to be "Minging", or crawling with germs? Do you recall the RSM's Drill Parades, when even the Instructors got inspected-by the "TARA" before you did? The wearing of full Green Duty Order from the 12th (the week I changed cap badges) to the 14th week of training and then full White Duty Order from then until pass out. Do you also recall the AKC cinema, called the Globe, which was surrounded by pathways made of black clinker and cinders? We were once inspected by our Squad Officer, a Lt Peter Mason, who found a microscopic piece of Proberts Whitening on one of the inside brasses of my pistol holster. Sgt Fred Fletcher made me, and all the other "naughty" boys lay our white kit on the wet black clinker and then made the whole Squad carry out a drill sequence over the top of our gear. The final punishment was to parade with all kit rewhitened and immaculate, at the Guardroom at 1300 hours. No NAAFI break and lunch that day! You couldn't borrow other blokes' kit, because all items were stamped with your Army Number. Harry Burden was the RSM when I was a Probationer, yes, we were that and not Recruits, and Harry was God! He once put a Post Office Telegraph Boy in the "Nick" because he cycled onto Harry's Square when he was faking a pass out parade rehearsal. I was once put in the cells because I stepped on to the Square when he was taking a Junior Officers drill parade. I'd been told to report to A Company office and had raced through the Main Block ground floor corridor and onto the square without looking fist. I was going to pick up a 36-hour leave pass, but that went "for a Burton" as two Regimental Police LCpls double marched me off to the cells. The Depot was alive with Probationers as in those days of National Service, drafts of 200-400 men a fortnight were sent to the Depot and Training Establishment RMP (many against their will) to train as Military Policemen. Most had only served 2-4 weeks in their initial units, and the majority went on to happily do their two years as RMP NCOs, God bless them. Many Probationers never made it to pass out and could get to the last week of training before being RTU'd. Added to this throng of young men were guys coming back to the Depot for further postings or to finish their National Service, and you can imagine how full the place got. Females of the WRAC Provost were not trained at Inkerman; they had their own training facility at Guildford. I remember hearing that that men and women later trained together at Chichester, and even drilled together!!!!! I still can't get my head around that.

A BRIEF HISTORY OF INKERMAN BARRACKS, KNAPHILL

MY GREAT UNKNOWN/COMPLETELY UNEXPECTED ASSET

From a very early age my late father considered I had not inherited his many great assets and that as far as 'school and life thereafter' were concerned, I would never be more than a 'Plodder' and as a result he took no further interest in my advancement once I had arrived at St. Bartholomew's Grammar School, Newbury.

On my arrival at Newbury Police Station at 0600 hours on a miserable February morning on my first day as a 'Civilian Clerk' with the Berkshire Constabulary in February 1948, the Duty Sergeant, Sergeant Frederick COSTAR, informed me I would have to teach myself to type straight away. I had met Sergeant Costar previously as his wife had been brought up in the Council Houses in East Ilsley and had later become one of my father's teachers at the East Ilsley Elementary School where he was Headmaster. Sergeant Costar was in the habit of spending his Summer Annual Leave with his in-laws and whilst doing so drove a tractor for Maurice WILSON, a local farmer, during the 'Harvest Season'. The Sergeant was over 6ft tall, 17 stone in weight and turned out to be a 'Brute of a Man' both on and off duty, completely lacking any form or kindness or sympathy especially as far as I was concerned.

During my first week I was placed in front of a very old Oliver three bank typewriter and told to get on with it. I started gingerly with the index finger on the right hand but whenever Costar found me doing this he would strike the back of my left hand with an ebony ruler, which proved very painful, and tell me to use both hands. Fortunately, owing to his shift pattern our paths only crossed one week in three.

By the time I was moved from Newbury to Wokingham in August 1948, I had become quite fast and accurate both on a typewriter and a teleprinter and as a result very popular amongst the Constables at Newbury for typing out their reports for a small financial gain.

In August 1949 Superintendent Chandler, Divisional Commander at Wokingham, moved me from General Duties as a Uniform Cadet to a Plain Clothes General Clerk position with the CID, where my duties included typing out extensive legal files for submission to Solicitors/Director of Public Prosecutions. On a number of occasions at Wokingham I was congratulated on my accuracy on the typewriter.

In January 1950 I was called up for National Service in the Wiltshire Regiment at Bulford passed as A1 as far as fitness was concerned, but with a note on my file that I should not be given a 'Sedentary job' after training owing to my weight. After six weeks' 'Infantry Training' I was transferred from the Wiltshire Regiment to the Royal Military Police and posted to Inkerman Barracks, Woking for 16 weeks' training. Towards the end of my training at Woking, 30 of my intake, including me, were sent to the Royal Army Ordnance Corps Barracks, Badajos Barracks, Aldershot on a four-week Clerks Course with the Bomb Disposal Group. Why the Bomb Disposal Group I will never understand! Included in the 'Training' was a Pitmans Typing Course – there we were learning to type with a musical background in a room, dressed in full uniform complete with white belt and gaiters together with Hobnail Boots, for hours on end learning the art of 'Touch Typing'. At the end of the course we had to take a 'Test' conducted by a RAOC Corporal. When the 'Test' was completed, I was called into another room by the Corporal and told in private that he had a problem with me, i.e. I was "a useless 'Touch Typist' but by far the fastest and most accurate in the class. You will take the 'Test' again in private and during same I will go out of the room." I carried out the test in my 'self taught manner'. I was still the most accurate and by far the fastest in the class. The Corporal said, "You have passed with flying colours – that will cost you a packet of Senior Service cigarettes please."

At the end of the course with the RAOC I returned to lnkerman to complete my basic training at the end of which I was posted to the 'Main Orderly Room' at lnkerman as a Clerk on the 'Permanent Staff' and told to report to the Chief Clerk. All Regiments and Corps have a Headquarters in the UK. lnkerman Barracks was therefore the HQ for the RMP. Throughout the UK there were 'Combined Record Offices' which dealt with and kept all records of all personnel of about three or four groups. The RMP was grouped with three or four other Groups and based in Bournemouth.

lnkerman Barracks consisted of a Training Company (Average 1,200 in training at any one time with 'Intakes' about once a fortnight of an average of 150 who were split into three 'Squads' which trained for 12 weeks at lnkerman and four weeks at Aldershot and a Depot Company which held about 800 in transit at any one time). The Permanent Staff consisted of about 200 employed either in Training or keeping the Depot personnel under supervision. Whilst there was an Orderly Room in each Company, the main Orderly Room was over and above everyone else.

In every Corps or Regiment HQ there are two Clerks employed as either Part II/III Order Clerks covering all Officers within the whole Depot or 'Other Ranks' including Extra Regimental Employed. At Inkerman when I arrived on the 'Permanent Staff' the 'Task re Officers' was dealt with by a retired Captain and the 'Other Ranks' post had become vacant. Because of my obvious expertise in typing I was given the 'Other Ranks' post.

The Main Orderly Room Staff consisted of a Chief Clerk (seconded from the Military Staff Provost Corps – the Forces Prison Service), a Staff Sergeant Deputy in the RMP, four National Service Corporals and about 15 Lance Corporal Clerks. We all worked in 'Spider' accommodation with a main entrance and hall in the centre of the spider and two open plan rooms, one housing the Chief Clerk, Deputy Chief Clerk, the PART II/III Order Clerk, two corporals and two sections. The Chief Clerk had a private entrance near his desk. The other room housed filing, duplicators and other machinery operated by a number of Lance Corporals. At the end of this room there was a small room which housed the Duty Clerk at night to keep the whole outfit open 24/7. My small desk was situated immediately opposite The Chief Clerk/ Deputy Chief Clerk's long desk. I was therefore under their supervision the whole time.

The Commandant, a Lieutenant Colonel in the Irish Guards (there were no Commissioned Officers in the RMP when I was serving – they came from other Corps/Regiments. Some years afterwards the Corps had its own Commissioned Officers. All Commissioned Officers at the Depot were seconded from other Regiments and Corps) was housed in another Spider adjacent to The Orderly Room. This spider had its nearside overlooking the Orderly Room and directly in front of the window in front of my desk. I was therefore able to witness all movements on the staging which proved most interesting when the Commandant held his daily 'Disciplinary Orders' and all the offending soldiers were marched in to appear in front of the Commandant minus hat and belt. The Depot Adjutant, a Captain in the Welsh Guards, was also housed in this spider and the Regimental Sergeant Major visited daily to supervise the Disciplinary Parade.

About 0850 hours one weekday morning I witnessed a spectacle I have never forgotten. The Chief Clerk had not yet arrived for his daily duties but the Adjutant, a Captain in the Welsh Guards, came through the Chief Clerk's 'Private Door'; and sat in the Chief Clerk's chair. The Chief Clerk came in, complained about the Adjutant and returned to his Married Quarter. He did not return for three days after the Adjutant had been to the Married Quarter and apologised in person.

My work actually consisted of obtaining all data regarding all other ranks on the camp (e.g. movements, courses, sickness, promotions, disciplinary convictions – in fact, all data required by the Combined Record Office to be placed on the records held by the Combined Record Office. Having obtained the data, recorded same in a Register, I would then transfer the information to stencils every week which would be duplicated and the papers forwarded to the CRO.

After carrying out these duties to the apparent entire satisfaction of the Chief Clerk and the Combined Record Office Staff for about a year, I was promoted to the rank of Substantive Corporal and placed in charge of the 'Overseas Drafting Section' in the same room. This section's duties were to take possession of all the names of the RMP personnel 'Passing Out' from the Training Company and allocate them to 'Overseas Drafts' having been advised by the Combined Record Office of the vacancies to be filled around the whole world. We were also required to book passages on 'Troop Ships', for the personnel selected, regularly travelling from the UK to Hong Kong via the Med. BAOR (Germany etc) was considered as a 'Home Posting' – Home Postings within UK were dealt with by another Corporal and his team in the same room.

Towards the end of my two years' National Service I was promoted to the rank of Sergeant as the Chief Clerk of a Supplementary Reserve RMP Company. I was also offered, if I signed on as a 'Regular', a posting to the RMP Section, NATO, based in Paris with the promotion to Staff Sergeant.

For the last four months of my service I was 'going out' with Rachael COOMBES from West End, Chobham, Surrey, a very tall, slim, well groomed and elegant lady whom I had met during the weekly Dances held in the Gymnasium at Inkerman. She had visited Aunt May's at Crowthorne and had met with full approval. I was 'Demobbed' on the Thursday, remained within the Barracks until the following Tuesday, and of course met Rachael regularly. I reluctantly joined the Berkshire Constabulary at Reading HQ, on the Thursday, remained there until the following Friday until travelling to Folkestone for 16 weeks' training at the District Police Training Centre (allowed home for the weekend every four weeks). It must be said that all on my course were ex National Service and experienced great difficulty in settling down to civilian life, in fact one ex-Sailor could not resist being away from the sea for even a fortnight and resigned and returned.

On being posted to Ascot as a Probationer I experienced great difficulty in settling down and was literally off the rails. If I had not obtained an excellent record as a Police Cadet and done well in the RMP, I would not have had my Probation confirmed. Having met Gwen again in 1953 and being granted the post of Sub-Divisional Clerk/Court Officer which I enjoyed for nine years, I would never have carried on in the Police Service. On looking back, I am far more proud of my record in the RMP than I have ever been of the Police Service.

After about a couple of months both Rachael and I realised that our relationship could not continue owing to distance problems and she decided to take up a career in Nursing, commencing her training at St. Richards Hospital, Chichester. Although I have never seen her since, she did visit Aunt May one Sunday to explain the full situation which Aunt May fully accepted. A few months later I met up with Gwen again having not seen her since January 1950 and a very happy life ensued for both of us.

MEMORIES OF PC 309 RICHARD ALLEN, BERKSHIRE CONSTABULARY

In April 1957 I was posted from Ascot to Bracknell and allocated a very ancient house attached to the original Bracknell Police Station (long demolished) situated at the West End of Bracknell High Street. The two properties were linked by a Cell Passage (four cells) with a cell door complete with a very large key facing into our Hall.

A short period after my daughter was born in October 1958, I was appointed an 'Acting Sergeant' for a period of six months and proudly wore two chevrons on one arm only. One evening in 1959 during the 'Rush Hour' I found myself entirely on my own (still as an Acting Sergeant) attending a serious road traffic accident in Binfield Road, Bracknell between a private car and a taxi. The damage was extensive and the injuries moderate. On my arrival I found the driver of the car, a Chief of Security Officer at a Bracknell Factory, under the influence of alcohol but lying on the ground having suffered a severe blow in the face inflicted by the taxi driver. I arrested both, took them to the Police Station and called the doctor. More about this incident later.

One morning in 1959 I was meeting a Constable at a 'Conference Point' in High Street, Bracknell outside the Post Office when I collapsed on the pavement. I managed to get to my feet and with the help of the Constable staggered back to the Bracknell Police Station which was only a few hundred yards from the Post Office. My doctor was called and diagnosed 'Asian Flu'. He instructed me to retire to bed and stay there in isolation with only my wife and daughter in the house.

After a few days a typewriter was delivered to my wife, together with an unfinished file regarding the aforesaid traffic accident, a packet of A4 paper and instructions from my Chief Inspector that as soon as practicable I must complete this file at home in order that it could be submitted to Force Headquarters for consideration of proceedings after the necessary legal advice had been obtained.

I did manage to complete the file on the kitchen table, and after a fortnight sick returned to work on 'Light Duties' (I never resumed my role as Acting Sergeant) which lasted for about five months during which I lost four stone in weight.

A decision of 'No further action' was eventually arrived at on the file and the two persons arrested were informed.

Just before Christmas 1959 a case of wine/spirits was delivered to my Police House by a local off licence apparently ordered by the Chief Security Officer involved in the accident. I immediately informed my Chief Inspector who told me to take the case back to the Factory Gate without delay and get a signature for the case which was duly carried out.

Shortly after Christmas 1959 I was informed by my Chief Inspector, Herbert John SNOWLEY, that Sergeant George YULE, stationed at Ascot, had made a complaint to the Chief Constable that he was in an off-licence in Bracknell when he witnessed the purchase of the case of alcohol by the said Chief Security Officer who had requested that the case be delivered to me personally at my house – in other words YULE had made an allegation of corruption against me. Fortunately, my Chief Inspector was able to give a complete satisfactory explanation regarding the whole matter. A full investigation, however, did take place which completely exonerated me but revealed that both Sergeant Yule and the Chief Security Officer were involved with 'extra-marital affairs' with the same single woman, namely a WPC based at Wokingham.

'The Charabanc'

In 1953 I was one of eight young Constables serving at Ascot, Berkshire and housed in rather primitive conditions in accommodation in an old Police Station in the High Street. It so happens that I had just been the first single Constable to purchase a motor car, namely a standard 14 saloon, 1933 model with a free wheel gear box. The fact that I had a motor car, nicknamed the charabanc, caused a certain amount of envy amongst the personnel at Ascot. At the time of this story I was engaged on uniform cycle patrol in the area from 0600 hours to 1400 hours, retired to bed at about 2230 hours intending to rise about 0445 hours, to enable me to report for briefing at 0545 hours. At about 0130 hours I was awakened by Constable Benjamin Plant, the Station Duty Officer. This was not unusual at the time as the single men were often called out at night whilst off duty to attend some incident or other. (There was no financial remuneration to cover such duties in those days, it was considered part of the job. If you were going out off duty you even had to inform the station where you were going.) Constable

Plant informed me that a young, very attractive lady, had just alighted from the last Green Line coach from Victoria at Ascot and had found herself completely stranded as she had intended to get to Bracknell four miles down the road. Being unattached at the time, I quickly got out of bed, dressed in sports jacket, collar and tie etc, which was the custom at the time, walked about a quarter of a mile to the Police Garage where the car was housed, unlocked the garage and drove the car to the front of the Police Station. On entering the public area, I had quite a shock. The young attractive lady was in fact an eighty-year-old woman dressed from hat to toe in black with a very heavy suitcase. Such was the situation that I could not state my true feelings to Constable Plant. I had no alternative but to 'bear a stiff upper lip', open the car door, place the lady in her seat and store the suitcase in the boot. On reaching Bracknell High Street I stopped the car, but the lady refused to get out, stating she wanted to go a few hundred yards further. I did as I was told, removed the luggage from the boot and wished her well. At this stage she duly produced a two shilling tip. By this time feeling rather sorry for the old lady who was obviously not well off financially, I said to her "no, I cannot accept the tip it was the least I could do". She immediately without any hesitation produced a rolled umbrella and started hitting me around the head, causing a few minor injuries. I thought it better to leave the matter and not arrest her.

Some weeks later I went down to the police garage to collect my car one sunny afternoon, got into the car and tried to start it up. Almost immediately there was a very loud explosion with dense black smoke everywhere. I got out of the car only to see a number of Police Officers in uniform led by Chief Inspector 'Taffy' Evans heading for the garage to investigate the explosion. On getting under the car we found that the whole of the exhaust system was just one flat piece of tin – someone had placed a potato in the rear of the exhaust pipe. The Chief Inspector was speechless, as he was a few months later when he entered his office one morning and found the whole of his office, adjacent to the main entrance, adorned with various beautiful flowers/ plants etc. They had apparently been placed there by a number of very attractive young Italian ladies who were known to the 'Single Men' and employed in the area as 'Au Pairs'.

RMA Sandhurst Ball – 1956

Whilst at Ascot and just after marriage to Gwen, I was asked to arrange an outing to the Wokingham Division Police Ball held in the Gymnasium at RMA Sandhurst. I booked a coach from White Services, Windsor Great Park. The coach was full, but Inspector DEDMAN decided to make his own way with his wife in his Morris 10-4, BKJ 776.

The Ball took place within the main part of the Gymnasium and the side rooms housed the VIP Guests, Police Bar, Public Bar, Public Rest Room, Orchestra Musicians Room etc. The main Orchestra was 'Joe LOSS' supported by the RMA Dance Orchestra.

All went well for the first two hours until it was reported to me that our driver from White Services, who was 'moonlighting' from the Thames Valley Bus Company, was in a state of intoxication in the Police Bar. When the Dance came to an end, it was found that the services of another Thames Valley Bus Driver, who was off duty at the Dance, had been obtained to drive the White Services Bus back to Ascot. Unfortunately, the other driver had gone home with the ignition key. My old friend Police Constable Peter EAST, well intoxicated himself, stated he knew how to start the coach and got busy winding baling wire around the spark plugs which of course was useless. Eventually the Coach was started with the aid of a penny. After we had gone a few miles, it was noticed that Inspector Dedman was following in his own car to ensure that no Police Officers were driving the said coach. Next morning Inspector Dedman received a telephone call from the Manager of the Ascot Site of Thames Valley Bus Company complaining that when one of his drivers arrived to take the first bus out at 0630 hours he was drunk and not in a state to drive the bus. Somehow Dedman dealt satisfactorily with the complaint there and then and nothing further was heard of the matter.

BERTRAM MILLS CIRCUS – Circa 1956

PC258 Patten was riding his motorcycle in High Street, Ascot when he saw a Bertram Mills Animal Trainer exercising a full-grown tiger on the pavement near a mother with her little girl. He stopped to see if everything was OK. The Trainer then took the tiger on a lead to the Police Station (now The Old Court House). Being on duty at the time I walked into the main office to see Walter SCOTT (an old war Reserve) in a rather shocked state trying to deal with the Trainer and tiger. About a month later a letter was received at Ascot Police Station from an irate American Lady in the USA just addressed to The Captain, Ascot City Police complaining about the incident involving the Trainer, tiger and little girl in the High Street.

Bertram Mills had their 'Winter Quarters' at South Ascot and whenever they went on tour they were taken through the High Street to the Railway Station to board the Goods Train conveying them to different parts of the UK. Residents en route (including Police Personnel) made quick use of the many 'Deposits' from the elephants by collecting same in buckets and digging it into their gardens/allotments.

At the same time Billy Smarts Circus had their 'Winter Quarters' in North Street, Winkfield which resulted in a number of incidents such escaping monkeys etc.

THE UNUSUAL HOUSE BREAKER – Circa 1958 – Bracknell

During my period as a Sub-Divisional Clerk/Court Officer at Bracknell 1957-1961 with duties 0900 to 1300 and 1400 to 1800 and being resident in a house attached to Bracknell Police Station I was required to answer and attend to all calls received when the office was closed between 2400 and 0800. This requirement was also shared with PC 233 TOWNSEND who resided in a detached Police House next to the Police Garage when he too was off duty at night (two weeks in three). These turn-outs averaged about three times a week.

At about 0030 hours one weekday I received a call from HQ that a male person had telephoned Reading Borough Police to say that he was standing at the top of Bracknell High Street and wished to confess to four housebreakings that he had just committed. I got dressed, got the Austin A40 Police car out of the garage and went up the High

Street where I found the said man. He stated he had just broken into four houses. As I did not believe him, he then took me to each of the four houses where we awakened the occupants and introduced their burglar to them. In each case he had broken in and stolen a small amount. I then asked him if that was that, to which he replied, "I have also broken into Smiths Newsagents at Bracknell Railway Station." He had, and I then took him to Wokingham and charged him with all the offences. He later pleaded 'Guilty' at Berkshire Quarter Sessions at Newbury, stating that he had committed the offences to spite his wife whom he had fallen out with. He was given two years' imprisonment. Three years later he did the self same thing in Henley for the same reason, for which he received further imprisonment. I was called to the second hearing to give evidence of the first offence. I made my mark at this hearing by being late, having been held up in traffic. On coming through the Wharf Car Park I was greeted by Counsel in the street in a state of agitation and quickly escorted into the Court where the Judge was awaiting my presence with some irritation.

Our Police House at Bracknell had an internal door to the Police Station. A large cell door with a huge key. On opening the door you came to a cell passage, passing four cells before you came to another large cell door beyond which was the General Office.

Louise was born on 15th October 1958 and shortly after her birth the whole country was hit by an Asian Flu Pandemic. Just before we left Bracknell, Louise made her presence felt by opening the side gate, going along the street to a huge new roundabout and stopping all the traffic thereon. Fortunately, she was recovered safely without a scratch. A lesson to us all!

One weekday morning my Chief Inspector decided to take me and another PC to a 'Blood Donating' Session in a Hall in Church Road. Shortly after leaving the Police Station three yobs started calling us names. The Chief Inspector, assisted by us, grabbed hold of the offenders and marched them up to the 'Session 'and informed them they would be released after they had each donated blood.

They readily agreed and were then released – nothing more being heard of the incident.

THE ERIC FULLBROOK CASE

Having been on 'Beat Duties' at Ascot for about a year and being over halfway through my period as a 'Probationary Constable', because of my previous experience in the force as a Police Cadet at both Newbury and Wokingham at a time when Cadets virtually carried out the same duties as a 'Civilian Clerk', I was selected to carry out the duties of Sub-Division Clerk/Court Officer at Ascot under the direct supervision of the 'Divisional Clerk Sergeant' at the Windsor Divisional Headquarters. As Sub-Division Clerk/Court Officer you were responsible for a variety of administrative tasks as far as the Sub-Division was concerned plus dealing with offences for prosecution from the time of authorisation of proceedings to the actual court hearing and the recording of results after proceedings. Included in these responsibilities were selecting witnesses, warning witnesses for court, greeting them at court, obtaining details of their expenses and acting as 'Court Usher'.

In the event of a conviction, fines would normally be collected by the Magistrates' Clerk's Assistant at the court. Should the defendant be given time to pay by the magistrates and fail to do so within the stated period, a warrant for the defendant's arrest would be issued for non-payment of fine. On the execution of the warrant by a Police Officer, the defendant would either hand over the necessary monies or be arrested and bailed to appear before the magistrates. Should the Police Officer be handed the necessary monies, he would then issue a receipt from his personal receipt book to the defendant and later hand the said monies to the Sub-Division Clerk who would endorse receipt in the personal receipt book, take over the monies, and make the necessary entry in a ledger kept for the purpose. At the first available date the monies would then be handed to the Clerk to the Magistrates who would then acknowledge receipt in the ledger.

After carrying out the above duties for about a year and dealing with the same Magistrates Court Clerk, namely Eric FULLBROOK, who, apart from being the Clerk of the Windsor County Magistrates Court was also Clerk to the Wokingham Magistrates Court and Reading County Magistrates Court, the Berkshire Constabulary underwent a re-organisation which placed the Ascot Sub-Division under the Wokingham Division.

I quickly realised that Eric FULLBROOK, whose main office was in Wokingham, was on somewhat friendly terms with my new Superintendent to the extent they travelled together on Saturdays to watch home games at nearby Reading Football Club.

After paying over significant amounts of cash to Eric Fullbrook, I became concerned over the actual system and the possible casual attitude in which they were received. I mentioned it to my then Chief Inspector who immediately dismissed my concerns. Later my Chief Inspector was replaced by an Inspector. I also began to notice that FULLBROOK appeared to be somewhat hostile to me on occasions during my duties, especially when acting as Court Usher. These thoughts were confirmed when my new Superintendent warned me to be very careful when dealing with FULLBROOK as he had gathered from casual conversation with FULLBROOK that FULLBROOK did not consider me to be efficient in my duties.

Shortly after my conversation with the Superintendent, in 1954 the Force experienced a change of Chief Constable. Whilst the new Chief Constable was settling in, he visited all stations within the Force. As far as Ascot was concerned, he visited on a number of occasions mainly because of the presence of the Ascot Racecourse. On one visit, whilst I was acting as Court Usher and FULBROOK was taking the court, the Chief Constable came and stood at the back of the court for some time viewing all the proceedings with great interest. During this time a well-known 'male troublemaker' caused a disturbance whilst being dealt with for a minor offence and the magistrates instructed me to remove him from the court. I started carrying out the instruction in a very caring manner in view of the Chief Constable's presence. To my utter amazement, the Chief Constable immediately took over the task from me, kicked the offender up the backside and sent him flying through the exit doors with great speed. He then turned to me and said, "And that is the manner you should have dealt with him." I heard no more about the incident from either the Chief Constable or the Magistrates Clerk and it must be stated I had no further problems with Fullbrook at that stage of my service.

In April 1957 it was decided, owing to the growth of Bracknell New Town, to revert Ascot to a 'Section Station', elevate Bracknell to a Sub-Divisional Headquarters, placing it under the command of a newly promoted Chief Inspector, and moving me and my office to Bracknell. As a result, the Court House at Ascot was closed down and the Windsor County Magistrates Court was re-located in the Offices of the Easthampstead Rural District Council in Bracknell.

The Magistrates Court continued as before under the continued direction of Eric FULLBROOK. All appeared to go well until December 1960.

At the court immediately before the Christmas Festival, I attended the court in my usual capacity together with the Chief Inspector who had regularly prosecuted at the court since the move to Bracknell. FULLBROOK arrived and immediately approached the Chief Inspector and said, "Do you think PC Allen could collect the fines today as my assistant is unable to attend", to which the Chief Inspector readily agreed and instructed me accordingly. During the morning two male defendants appeared before the magistrates on the charge of 'publishing indecent photographs'. They both pleaded guilty and both were fined the sum of £25. After the court hearing I collected the sum of £50 in five-pound notes and at the end of the day handed FULLBROOK the cash. As he was acknowledging receipt in the ledger he said, "That's a nice Christmas present." I took this as a jovial festive remark and made no comment.

A few weeks after the above Court, I was carrying out the duties of Station Duty Officer one afternoon at Bracknell when in came the above two defendants who appeared to be very irate. They greeted me with the comment, "We both gave you £25 in cash at the Court and now we find that there is a warrant for our arrest for non-payment of fine. Explain yourself." I did the best to explain myself and referred them to the Magistrates Clerk's office at Wokingham.

Being greatly concerned about the above matter and the fact my Chief Inspector was non-contactable on Rest Day, I immediately telephoned my immediate supervisor, the Divisional Clerk Sergeant at DHQ Wokingham who immediately put the Superintendent in the picture. Next morning my Chief Inspector returned to duty and remonstrated with me over my action the previous day and the fact I had not kept him in the picture regarding the allegation. I heard nothing further on the matter from any source until 1962, approximately 18 months later. In the meantime, my Chief Inspector at Bracknell had been promoted to the rank of Superintendent and appointed Divisional Commander of the Abingdon Division and I had been promoted to the rank of Sergeant and appointed Divisional Clerk Sergeant of the Abingdon Division, both working out of Abingdon Police Station.

During the autumn of 1962 I was on leave and with my wife and children visiting my parents in Sunninghill, Berkshire, and on embarking on our return journey to Abingdon we decided to call in on her parents who resided in Wokingham. We had not been at Wokingham long when a Berkshire Constabulary Mobile Crew, well known to me, came speeding up the drive. I spoke to the driver who said, "Your very irate father has just called Wokingham Police Station from a telephone box at Sunninghill and forcibly requested your immediate return to Sunninghill as a Detective Superintendent from New Scotland Yard is in the house and has demanded your presence, but will not give a reason for his visit."

I immediately left my family at Wokingham and returned to Sunninghill in a manner of great urgency. On arrival at Sunninghill I found my father (a retired Headmaster who shortly after died of cancer) in a very sorry state. He immediately informed me that the Detective Superintendent could wait for my return no longer and had returned to London, still refusing to state the reason for his visit. My father had unfortunately gained the wrong impression that I was in some form of serious trouble and it became almost impossible to pacify either him or my mother. I must state that my wife and in-laws were not impressed either.

I returned to my duties at Abingdon the next day and immediately acquainted my Superintendent of the events of the previous day. He admitted that the Detective Superintendent had enquired of my whereabouts, would not disclose the reason, and would be arriving at Abingdon after lunch to interview me. Having thought in depth about the matter overnight I could only come to the conclusion it could be something to do with FULLBROOK's past actions. I reminded the Superintendent of the situation at Bracknell with FULLBROOK during 1960/1961 and the fact that he had remonstrated with me over my actions at the time. To my utter amazement, he denied all knowledge of any such matters and I immediately realised that 'I had been left on my own' to deal with any subsequent enquiry.

The Detective Superintendent from the Yard arrived and for some hours interrogated me at length, at the end of which he took a two-page statement from me. After I had signed the statement he put all his papers in a briefcase and said, "Now I have closed the official interview, tell me what really happened. I am sure you know far more about this matter than is included in your statement." I assured him he had had the full story and he then departed for London. From that date I did not discuss the visit with anyone as it was obvious this would lead to problems.

In November 1962 a teleprinter message was circulated around the force to the effect that I was being posted to Force Headquarters, Sulhamstead, as a Sergeant in the Administrative Department and a house had been allocated to me on South Drive.

I let it be known that I was not happy with the posting for a number of reasons, but was advised that it was important for me to take the post to enhance my future career. I reluctantly took up the post on 3rd December 1962 which lasted until May 1964 when the Chief Constable decided I should gain more 'Operational Experience and posted me to Wantage. I objected to Wantage (another long story) and the posting was changed to ' Country Sergeant at Wallingford (the only Sergeant) to police the Borough and five villages with the assistance of ten constables – which meant a 24/6 hour responsibility for me.

During the summer of 1963 I had a 'Witness Summons' served upon me to attend the Reading Borough Magistrates Court, along with another Constable who had been Court Officer at the Reading County Magistrates Court, a Magistrates Clerk from a court in Southern

England who had appeared in front of one of Fullbrook's courts and found guilty and fined for driving a motor car without due care and attention and over 30 other witnesses. This was the first time I had heard anything whatsoever about the investigation since being interviewed at Abingdon. Certainly no member of the Force had approached the subject with me in any form.

The day before the committal hearing I was summoned to the Deputy Chief Constable's Office when he said to me, "I would not be in your shoes for all the tea in China – watch your back. I am arranging for you and the other Constable involved in this case, to be accompanied from this Headquarters to the court hearing, throughout the hearing and return to this Headquarters by the Force's Detective Superintendent. You will both stick to him like glue at all times and never leave his presence." The Deputy Chief Constable's instructions were adhered to, no incidents occurred and FULLBROOK was committed for trial at the Number One Court of the Old Bailey in London.

The days of the hearing at the Old Bailey arrived. The Deputy Chief Constable made exactly the same statement to us again and gave the same instructions. FULLBROOK pleaded 'Not Guilty' to all charges and was defended vigorously by Learned Counsel. The trial lasted for weeks but after I gave evidence he dismissed his Learned Counsel and defended himself. The jury found him guilty and sentenced him to three years' imprisonment.

During my time in the Witness Box, I stood firm to very heavy interrogation. At one stage of my evidence I was asked by Defence Counsel, "You have known the defendant for many years, do you consider him to be the type of person to commit the offences as charged?" I stood in silence throughout these repeated questions. After the question had been repeated on a second occasion, the presiding judge came to my aid and said, "How on earth do you expect the Sergeant to answer that question?"

After FULLBROOK had served his imprisonment, he then appealed to a Tribunal for the return of his pension and I was again called to give evidence at the Tribunal. I was never acquainted of the result of his appeal.

SULHAMSTEAD STORIES

Just after the war and whilst at St. Barts, Newbury, I became very interested in photography having inherited from an uncle a 1920 116 camera and other equipment. At the same time the wife of a War Correspondent, namely Terry Ashwood, was evacuated to a nearby family in East Ilsley. Terry's peacetime career had been with 'Pathe Gazette News' and after the war he became Managing Director of the company and based in Wardour Street, London. After the war Terry offered me employment with the company but stated that the company could not employ me until after I had completed my National Service. For many reasons, the main one being that they could only offer me part-time employment in 1952 owing to financial difficulties within the industry, my employment did not come to fruition.

In February 1948 I left St. Barts, and obtained employment as a 'Boy Civilian Clerk' with the Berkshire Constabulary at the Police Station,

Pelican Lane, Newbury. As it happened Gwen obtained the employment as a Civilian Clerk at Wokingham Police Station and started work on the very same day. Little did I know at that stage that in six months I would become one of the first Police Cadets in the Force, forced to leave home because my parents decided at short notice to move to Wiltshire and had obtained a compassionate posting to Wokingham lodging with an aunt in Crowthorne. During my period of employment as a 'Boy', the Force Headquarters was situated at Abbey Street, Reading. After serving two years with first the Wiltshire Regiment and later with the RMP I returned to Abbey Street for a week and then went on to Sandgate.

My first Chief Constable was in fact Commander The Hon. Humphrey Legge, CVO, DSO, later the Earl of Dartmouth. Humphrey was a great character and beloved by the whole force throughout his life.

In 1948 The Chief Constable wrote to the Police Authority that HMI of Constabulary shared his view that the County Police Headquarters at Reading were obsolete and he asked the Standing Joint Committee to consider the possibility of acquiring for a new HQ Sulhamstead House, which he considered suitable if alterations were carried out. The residence then stood in extensive grounds of 125 acres but only 60 were retained for Police purposes, the remainder being sold as agricultural land.

The grounds in front of the mansion were laid out with two football pitches and a cricket square, and in addition there were also a bowling green, swimming pool and three hard tennis courts. A requirement for sporting facilities was therefore fully recognised and the members of the force themselves would contribute to 'the labour force' in their own time.

Speaking from memory I left for Sandgate on the first Sunday in February 1952, HM King George 6th died two days later, and the Berkshire HQ moved to Sulhamstead on 8th February 1952 being eventually officially opened on 24th May 1952. Humphrey officially retired in March 1954 and John Lovegrove WALDRON (a Wargrave, Berkshire man) who was later to become Sir John Waldron, Commissioner of the Metropolitan Police, took his place.

Circa Spring 1955 whilst serving as a Constable at Ascot and residing in very primitive single quarters, under the supervision of Inspector Reginald Dedman, an officer who had remained in the Force throughout the war and who was considered to be somewhat of an expert in the sport of cricket, I was summoned to his presence and informed that as I was on 'Rest Day' the following day and had no family commitments, I would accompany him to Sulhamstead on my Rest Day and spend the day assisting him to get the Cricket Pitch etc ready for the forthcoming season. He picked me up at 0800 in his private car, a 1934 Morris 10 index number BKK 4 76 and on arrival I spent the rest of the day mowing the cricket pitch and surrounding grass. At 0900 hours the following day I was again summoned to the Inspector's Office who said "I have had our Superintendent on the phone and he is not particularly happy. At about ten o'clock last night whilst at home he received a telephone call from the Chief Constable requesting that you be approached and asked whether you would be willing to move to Sulhamstead as a Constable and take on the task of Head Groundsman. The Superintendent stated that he told the Chief

Constable in no uncertain terms that you would not be interested." Later that day I was approached by a Constable with some 25 years' service whom I had known for some years and who happened to be the brother-in-law of my previous Superintendent who said, "Hello Dick it has come to my ears that you have turned down an offer for the post of Head Groundsman at Sulhamstead. You must be mad. If you had accepted that post you would shortly have been a Mobile Sergeant." Although I had passed the sergeants' examinations I was not promoted for another six years and in fact served at Bracknell for four years in the meantime.

In 1958 Waldron went on to the Met and Hodgson took over from Lancashire. In April 1961 I was promoted to Sergeant and posted to Abingdon as Divisional Clerk Sergeant.

Towards the end of November 1962 a teleprinter message was received stating that I would be posted to Headquarters Admin as a Sergeant with effect from 3rd December 1962. In fact I moved house on that date to 6, South Drive, Sulhamstead, my neighbours being the McGloin family whom I had served with at Bracknell. They proved to be excellent neighbours and did a great deal to settle down my wife and two young children.

On 5th December 1962 I reported for duty where I was greeted by Inspector William Hughes who spent the next hour instructing me in my future duties. The instruction went as follows:

1. Come with me to the Chief Constable's Office. You see that chair over there – place it under the clock behind the Chief Constable's

chair. Every morning at 0830 you will climb on to the chair, put the clock right to the second and turn the winding mechanism six times. Do not over wind. You will then place a new piece of white blotting paper on the pad on his desk and take the old piece down to your office and file it in date order. Bear in mind that in about three weeks' time the Chief Constable will remember he has written something down on the pad and will want to refer to it again.

2. On return to his office the Inspector continued with listing my responsibilities which included the following:

Safety and maintenance of the personal files relating to each member of the Force. I held the key.

Note:-As soon as practicable I took the opportunity to read my own file which proved to be most interesting in a number of ways, especially correspondence on the file with the Home Office regarding myself and the RMP.

On leaving full time service with the RMP, I was promoted to the rank of Sergeant and appointed the 'Chief Clerk' of a Provost Company within the RMP Supplementary Reserve for three years which required me to attend 14 days' annual camp in that position. Having been at Ascot on the beat for only a few weeks, I received a letter from the Home Office instructing me to attend camp during the last two weeks of June 1952. This of course clashed with Royal Ascot week. I submitted the usual report through which came back endorsed by the Chief Constable: 'Refused – you cannot leave your duties during Royal Ascot'.

I submitted another report stating that I would be considered 'absent without leave' if I did not report for the camp. I heard no more in writing but was later informed by my Superintendent that I had better report for annual camp as instructed by the Home Office. I found on my personal file that the Chief Constable had written to the Home Office stating that I could not be released from my duties as all leave, courses etc. within the force were cancelled during Royal Ascot and it was even more essential that Constable Allen was not away from the force as he was stationed at Ascot. The Home Office replied, "It is absolutely necessary for Sergeant Allen to attend training with his Provost Company as he holds the important post of 'Chief Clerk' of the company. The Chief Constable replied to the Home Office stating "If Constable Allen is so b---dy important to the British Army you had better keep him". I also attended camp the following two years but fortunately dates did not clash with Royal Ascot.

Compilation and distribution of Force Weekly Orders, Operation Orders for Ascot Races and Henley Regatta. Maintenance of files regarding 'State Occasions' at Windsor. This file was kept in a cardboard tube wrapped in black silk and tied up with black tape. Completing returns to the Home Office prior to a Government Inspection. House to House and Street Collection permits throughout Berkshire and many other responsibilities too long to list.

3. Stated that my times of duty were 0830-1300 and 1400-1730 Monday to Friday. 0800-1230 on Saturdays and report to Chief Constable in his office at 1000 hours every Christmas Day for one hour unless he had given permission for me to take my family away from Sulhamstead.

I was not informed until 1700 hours on the first day that all the admin staff were expected to carry out three hours a day, namely 1900-2200, voluntary overtime (no payment or time off in lieu) Mondays to Thursdays in order to catch up with their work not done during the day. Towards the end of my posting to Sulhamstead the following occurred which I have always found very interesting and included a tactic used by the HMI which I adopted in later life when necessary within my two main careers:

'Notice was received at HQ from the Home Office of a forthcoming Government Inspection which included the HMI's requirements on arrival. Amongst the many requirements the HMI stated that he did not wish all Headquarters staff to parade on the square to be inspected in what was then the traditional manner. Instead, he expected them to remain at their normal posts actually carrying out their normal duties. The day came, the HMI arrived in civilian clothes, and after coffee with the Chief Constable he was taken on a conducted tour of the staff. On arrival at the Admin Department our Superintendent was invited to introduce his staff to the HMI. When the party visited my desk, the Superintendent included the fact that he had an excellent staff who were quite willing to carry out 12 hours' voluntary overtime without compensation every week in order to remain on top of their workload. The HMI immediately seized on this point and started 'chatting up the Superintendent' in a most affable manner. The result of this was that the Superintendent came out with more and more home truths, having come to the conclusion the inspection was going extremely well. The HMI then continued his tour. All seemed to go well with the annual inspection throughout the Force. When the HMI's annual report was received by the Chief Constable and also the Standing Joint Committee, the following comment was included: 'There is something very wrong with management if it is necessary for staff to work regular overtime under normal circumstances. This should be rectified without delay'. Immediate action was taken within Headquarters and for the rest of my period at HQ we were not expected to work a minute over our normal time schedule.

The Inspector continued with his briefing to include the following:

1. As I had moved into 6, South Drive I could continue using the allotment in the grounds allocated to No. 6 to grow my vegetables etc. and the bench in the main greenhouse also allocated, to grow tomatoes and cucumbers. I would also be expected to keep up the very high standard demanded throughout the estate with respect to my own garden.

(Note: Whilst I was at HQ, the Deputy Chief Constable, Richard Baker, made it known that all his ripe tomatoes had been found missing and that a Senior Officer would be appointed to find the culprit. Inspector Dedman was duly appointed but was unable to ascertain the offender.)

Circa 2000 some forty years later I attended a Berkshire Reunion at Sulhamstead and during the afternoon I was amongst a group of retired officers of all ranks, including Reginald Dedman, now in his 92nd year, when the subject of the missing tomatoes arose. Reginald Dedman stated he was still cross over the matter and if he ever found the culprit he would most certainly hear about it. At this stage one of the party, a former senior officer of TVP (not me), made a full confession. To say the least, the outcome was hilarious and will be remembered by those present for a long time to come.

2. That only officers of the rank of inspector and above were allowed to enter the main entrance into Sulhamstead House either on or off duty, the remainder should always use the 'Tradesman's Entrance' at the rear of the building. (Note: It was most unfortunate at a later date when my daughter and a near neighbour's daughter, both aged five years at the time, were caught marking out a 'Hopscotch' frame in chalk on the tarmac outside the sacred front entrance. There was uproar!

3. Berkshire owned a 20-seater Bedford Duple coach which was mainly used to convey staff and families to and from Abbey Street, Reading, morning and evening. The HQ Garage personnel were instructed that every Thursday morning the coach should be used to pick up spare parts in Reading for the garage. At the same time wives residing on the estate could use this facility to shop in Reading which was very much appreciated as it could also include a visit to Heelas for coffee and meet up with old friends. It was stipulated, however, that the wives of Superintendents should be given the front seats in the coach, Inspectors' wives the next rows, the Sergeants' wives followed and the Constables' wives would sit at the back.

4. Children of school age were transported to their various schools by police transport.

At the end of this long first briefing Inspector Hughes said to me: "Do you fully understand everything – is there any questions?" To which I replied, "Yes all very interesting. There is one thing – they won't put me in the family way" to which he replied with a grin, "I should not be too sure about that". I then went to my desk thinking what have I got into – I never wanted to come near HQ in the first place.

At 2200 hours I completed my first day's work. Everybody got up including the Superintendent and Inspector and when I had cleared my desk I found all had disappeared. What I did not realise was that whilst the Superintendent and Inspector had left the building via the front entrance, all the others had left via patio doors into the garden and not via the main back entrance which was situated next to the Club Bar. In all innocence I proceeded towards the back door but unfortunately on passing the bar door I was waylaid by the Deputy Chief Constable who was having a quiet drink alone with the Duty Barman. At 0130 hours a very long interview was concluded and I made my way back via a shortcut through the woods to 6, South Drive. I regret I am unable to record the domestic reception. Suffice it to say that I was only on an annual salary of £900 with two children under five and wife as was the custom in those days, a full time housewife having just removed to a very remote area with nearest shop a mile away, a Doctors' Surgery four miles away, no public transport, an old Morris Oxford car and the start of the 1962/1963 very bad winter which continued until March making it necessary for a police snow plough/gritter endeavouring daily to make a passable route into Theale.

Although there was an excellent community spirit within the estate and socially we all got together, the work situation was difficult at times. It must be admitted, however, that on looking back with hindsight the whole experience was of great value to me in the future and I learned a great deal about man-management, which made life for me in future roles far more relaxed and more enjoyable.

After 18 months at Sulhamstead, I found myself posted to Wallingford as a 'Country Sergeant' on my own, looking after a borough and five villages for a period of three-plus years before promotion to Inspector in Charge of Woodley Sub-Division for only five months when, owing to the sudden death of the Deputy Chief Constable, I was seconded again to Sulhamstead to assist Supt. Tom Ingram to close down the force and attend the last meeting of the Standing Joint Committee with him whilst my senior colleagues were at Kidlington planning for the Thames Valley Constabulary.

During my time at Sulhamstead, apart from causing a stir within the community by going down with a serious case of mumps and as a result placed in isolation without any visitors, I witnessed the following incidents:

1. The late Norman Goodley, Training Sergeant at the time, setting light accidentally with a cigarette end a fully filled wastepaper basket which, being in flames, he threw out of the office window.

2. Quite frequently on a Saturday afternoon within the season, the local 'Hunt' used to exercise their right of way through the Sulhamstead House grounds, entering from the West Lodge entrance and exiting via the East entrance, causing damage to flower beds and grass verges en route. My neighbour, a PC, having

become extremely annoyed by the damage caused on these occasions, deliberately drove across the 'Hunt' from his garage, causing chaos with their progress. Nothing further was heard about this incident and during the remainder of my time there I cannot recollect the hunt taking the same route again.

3. The local farmer was prone to shooting rabbits at night time by using the headlights of his Land Rover whilst the vehicle was in motion.

4. As Christmas 1963 approached, the Chief Constable instructed me to include a paragraph in Force Weekly Orders to the effect that under no circumstances should Christmas presents be received at Police Stations or Police Houses within the Force from members of the public.

A few days before Christmas Mrs Barbara Hunt, Telephonist/Receptionist, asked me to attend Reception as she was experiencing difficulty with a member of the public dressed as a Gamekeeper over the above instruction. On arrival at Reception, I found an apparent Gamekeeper carrying two pheasants which he stated were for the Chief Constable. I immediately reported the visit to the Chief Constable in his office. The Chief Constable replied, "You know my policy over such matters, get rid of him." I returned to the reception and advised the caller of my Chief Constable's reaction, to which he replied, "I think he will receive these, they are with the compliments of Her Majesty the Queen." I returned to the Chief Constable with the pheasants and advised him of the situation. He made no further comment. Note: The following year at Wallingford I had to break the rule when a local

Magistrate dragged two large heavy barrels of sherry to the station. I informed the Magistrate of the Chief Constable's policy to which he replied, "How ridiculous! I and my family have taken this action over the past 40 years. Are you now going to refuse a well-meant tribute?" To cut a long story short, I accepted the sherry and then we disposed of it to a row of alms houses near to the station. They thoroughly enjoyed every drop.

5. Being a Sergeant in Admin I seemed to pick up tasks outside of my remit which no other member of staff wished to take on. One such task was Secretary to the Force Cricket Team, a sport of which I have no interest in. At the beginning of the 1963 cricket season I was informed that the previous Secretary had made all the arrangements for the coming season and I was handed a list of fixtures. The first two matches at home went off without a hitch. The next fixture did not go well, not being on the original list. At about 1400 hours on a Wednesday afternoon, George Barnes, a Civilian Clerk for many years in the Admin Office, drew my attention to a number of Berkshire and Reading Fire Brigade vehicles parked at the front of Sulhamstead House and a number of men dressed in white cricket gear in the pavilion. He said to me, "Is there a cricket match this afternoon?" to which I replied, "Not to my knowledge there is not a fixture listed for today". George replied, "You had better look out of the window." For the next hour George and I were chasing round the Headquarters trying to raise a team. By 1500 hours we had managed some form of opposition but not dressed in whites.

6. One of my many responsibilities was to carry out the local arrangements for the 'National Annual Police Examinations'. Shortly after arrival I retrieved the file on the subject and found that my predecessor had already booked the Olympia Dance Hall in Reading for the day, applications to sit from the force had been received, and times and date had been laid on nationally. Apparently, all I had to do was supervise the transport of desks etc. from Whiteknights Park, Reading to Olympia, arrange any catering necessary and ensure that all taking the exam together with invigilators were all aware of the arrangements. On the day before, together with Ben Webb (father of John Webb and caretaker at Sulhamstead at the time) and a one-ton van, the transportation was apparently completed. At 1730 the same day my Superintendent checked with me that all was well and asked me to confirm that the members of Reading Borough Police taking the exam had been catered for. The unfortunate answer was in the negative mainly because there was no mention of the requirement in the file, I had never been informed of any such arrangement and the thought never crossed my mind that we would be also catering for another force. The consequence of this fact resulted in Ben Webb and myself together with one-ton truck travelling to Whiteknights Park on the day, leaving at 0730 hours only to find no staff present and the stores locked and bolted. We found ourselves with no alternative but to literally break into the store to obtain the furniture. By 0845 (examination started at 0900) all was in place at Olympia and neither Ben Webb nor myself heard any more on the subject.

7. Force Standing Orders were always despatched from HQ on a Friday evening. Towards the end of 1963 HQ Staff were hit badly by a flu epidemic and I virtually found myself on my own in the office. I managed to get the Chief Constable's Secretary, Joyce Hiatt, to type out the orders and I had to use the old 'Gestetner' to print them. By 1500 the Orders were, I thought, ready for distribution until the Superintendent started to check them. He found two minor errors and instructed me that the mistakes should be amended and the orders be reprinted. I immediately told him I was reporting sick and went home, leaving the problem with him. The following day on returning to work (a Saturday morning) I found he had completed the whole task including distribution himself and nothing further was mentioned from any quarter.

In 1973 I was promoted to the rank of Superintendent in the Thames Valley Police and appointed Force Training Officer/Commandant TVP Training Centre with residence in a large detached house on site which in the Berkshire Constabulary days had been the Deputy Chief Constable's residence Whilst this proved to be a most enjoyable and rewarding period, the appointment only lasted until November 1974 when I was appointed Deputy Divisional Commander, Slough Division, residing in a detached Police House in Kendrick Road, Slough.

WALLINGFORD

During my first night at Wallingford I was called out of bed to a 'Burglary' at the house of the Senior Partner of Slade and Son, Solicitors, Wallingford, namely Roddy SLADE (who later became a great friend). On my arrival, much to my surprise, I was given a very warm welcome by Mr SLADE who quickly made it known to me that he was aware of the fact that I had only just been posted to Wallingford and even more surprising he was, in common with many other prominent 'Business Members of the Community', completely aware of my personal background.

On the first Saturday evening at Wallingford I was taken to the vicinity of the Town Hall, Wallingford by one of my ten Constables, namely PC 322 ELWELL, a Constable I had previously known as he had joined the Berkshire Constabulary just after me and who prior to joining had been a Sergeant in the Coldstream Guards. Standing on the steps, he introduced me to the local 'yobs' and warned them strongly regarding their future behaviour whilst on my 'patch'. They listened to him intently with no comment, no doubt caused by the fact that at that time I was seven foot tall with my helmet on and well built. During my time at Wallingford I experienced very little problem with the locals and in fact when we were invaded by a neighbouring gang from Berinsfield they greatly assisted me and my officers in keeping order usually with the comment 'Do not come over here upsetting our Sergeant'.

My period at Wallingford from May 1964 to August 1967 proved to be a very happy and rewarding one for me, my wife Gwen and my two children Louise and Nicholas, despite the fact that I was on constant call 24 hours a day, six days a week, and the only Sergeant at Wallingford covering the Town, Cholsey, Moulsford, North Moreton, South Moreton, Long Wittenham, Little Wittenham and Brightwell-cum-Sotwell.

On arrival at Wallingford I had not yet been successful with my 'Inspectors Examination' and was quite content with my lot. The Chief Constable, Charles HODGSON, was not happy with my situation and after about two weeks came to see me at Wallingford on a number of matters including my future in the Force and at the end of the interview issued the following ultimatum: "You are not staying at Wallingford for the rest of your service. If you pass your examination, I will promote you within six weeks. If you do not, you will be posted to Faringdon immediately. I passed the examination in February 1967 and was promoted to Inspector in charge of the Woodley Sub-Division, seven months later amalgamation arrived and he again promoted me to the rank of Chief Inspector at Bracknell.

My Constables at Wallingford ranged from very experienced 'second world war veterans' to probationers and all proved to be very loyal and generally hard working. One Constable, however, PC 52 Gordon Bartlett, was always outstanding in smartness of dress and loyalty to the extent his boots were always, despite the weather, highly polished, his trousers always pressed and his handwriting copperplate. He dealt with literally everything in a meticulous manner although slow and determined. During this period it must be appreciated that there were no mobile phones or other immediate means of communication other than residential telephones, telephone kiosks and radios fitted in some police vehicles. Officers made 'Conference Points' outside telephone kiosks at pre-arranged times On one occasion PC Bartlett was on cycle patrol in Long Wittenham when he received information from a member of the public that an old lady resident had not been seen for some time and was a cause for concern. PC Bartlett went to the house but was unable to raise any reply by normal means. He then borrowed a ladder and climbed to the bedroom window, saw the lady in bed apparently ill, climbed in the window and endeavoured to attend to her needs. Back at the station we knew nothing of this incident, but after a time became concerned because we were unable to contact him. Towards the end of his tour of duty, such was our concern that we started to search for him. He was eventually found still caring for the woman. All ended well and the lady survived.

On another occasion PC Bartlett was sent to deal with a fatality on the railway line at Cholsey. On arrival he found the body in a state of decapitation with its head some distance from the body. He supervised the removal of the body and laid it out in the mortuary. In due course PC Bartlett was called upon by HM Coroner to prepare for an Inquest, i.e. arrange for a Jury, warn witnesses to attend and of course arrange suitable accommodation. Whilst preparing the room he called the station with a request for a blackboard, easel and chalk (a most unusual request for an Inquest). When everyone concerned with the Inquest arrived (including me) we found he had drawn a complete plan of the site of the disaster entirely to scale on the blackboard. When he gave evidence, duly armed with a pointer, he caused great interest to everyone present with his very detailed description of the whole matter.

One Sunday afternoon I was quietly resting in bed after being very late on duty on the Saturday when Gwen received a call from PC Bartlett who was carrying out the duties of Station Duty Officer. He stated he wished to speak to me regarding closing the Police Station for a short while. Gwen refused the request and insisted to hear why he had to close the station. He eventually came up with the reason saying "A man has just called into the station with blood pouring from his trousers after catching a certain part of his anatomy in the zip fastener". Gordon Bartlett considered it would be much quicker to get the van out and take the patient to a nearby cottage hospital than call an ambulance. The task was duly carried out and the man survived. He was equally meticulous with family matters. Whenever his car went into a garage for service, he always took a stool on which he could sit and supervise every movement of the mechanic whilst the car was being serviced. On another occasion he was taking his family on holiday to the Isle of Wight in the car. To ensure there were no problems with the travel arrangements and the family were on time leaving Brightwell, he decided to have a full rehearsal the previous day of loading the car and passengers in the car, duly timing the whole thing. The next day his alarm did not go off as planned and they missed the Ferry to the Isle of Wight. There were many more incidents with this officer during my time at Wallingford, too many to list now.

During my time at Wallingford we were blessed with a very popular Lady Mayor, known by everyone as 'Topsy'. Her husband, employed by the AERE, Harwell, was equally popular and also greatly involved with the community. Every Christmas morning she would visit many establishments within the Borough, which of course included the Police Station. A small buffet, with suitable drinks, was always laid out on the Sergeant's table and a good festive time was had by all. Later in the day we would deliver any 'bottles' brought to the Police Station to the residents of local 'Alms Houses'. After the 'Reception', my staff would then adjourn to the 'Sergeant's Police Accommodation' for a further festive gathering. On New Year's Eve there would be again 'Open House' available at my accommodation duly hosted by

Gwen. New Year's Eve was always a very busy time for us with the usual incidents. From 2345 to 0015 I would arrange for the main road through the town to be closed to traffic in order that the' Wallingford Citizens' could celebrate the occasion with an 'Extensive Conga Dance' through the Market Place and adjoining streets. On one occasion when the road was being re-opened to traffic, I saw a very wealthy gentleman with his Rolls-Royce waiting patiently at the traffic lights at the Lamb Cross Roads. I apologised profusely to him for the holdup, but he immediately assured me that he and his passengers had enjoyed every minute. He said, "We have had a terrible meal and evening at a restaurant just outside Wallingford and the celebrations at Wallingford really made us forget the experience and really enjoy the atmosphere in the Town Centre."

On one occasion I was enjoying dinner with my family when at about 1830 I received a telephone call from the Deputy Mayor, Doctor Charles WILKINSON, an excellent doctor, very 'Community Orientated' and a neighbour of Agatha Christie who said, "At 6.00pm we commenced a 'Banquet' at the Town Hall in order to celebrate Alderman Alfred LESTER's long time very valuable service to the Borough by presenting him with the 'Freedom of the Borough of Wallingford'. As he was getting on in years the Mayor decided to carry out the presentation immediately before the meal commenced. Sadly as he was being presented with the award he suddenly passed away. I have pronounced life extinct and informed HM Coroner. I regret you must come along now and carry out your official duties. Obviously all guests have been asked to leave which now causes a great problem as to how we should dispose of the food and drink and your opinion/action over the matter would be very well welcome." I immediately attended and carried out my sad duties and we distributed all the food and drink around the 'Alms Houses' in the Town. The whole action taken took us right through to about 2300 hours when it was decided that after such a sad evening we should all relax at a 'Lock In' at the Rowbarge Public House. The Deputy Mayor, the Undertaker, the Hearse Driver, other citizens who had been directly involved in the aftermath, and of course myself and other officers, then accepted the generous hospitality of the Landlord.

The Didcot Magistrates sat at the Town Hall once a month. On one occasion I was in attendance as a witness in a case of 'taking and driving away a car without the owner's consent' against a male person aged about 20 years who had pleaded 'Not Guilty'. I had given evidence, was still present in the court and it came to the point when the defendant was given the opportunity to make a statement on the witness stand. No sooner had he started making his statement when his attitude changed to one of great hostility which caused him to jump out of the box and climb on to the magistrates bench and kick the magistrates. I immediately leaped into action, getting hold of his arm, swinging him into the air and landing on top of him on the floor. Blood was pouring from his face. The Chairman immediately ordered me to take him downstairs and clean him up. I duly carried out the instruction and returned to the Court with the defendant. He had suffered minor injuries and I had sustained a sprained ankle and the buttons had been torn from my tunic. The Chairman then said, "We will now carry on with the case as though nothing has happened." The defendant was found guilty of the original offence. I duly submitted a report to my Chief Constable regarding the whole incident which was later returned endorsed with the comment "Injury duly noted

– perhaps Mrs Allen could sew on the buttons on your tunic". End of matter.

Whilst stationed at Wallingford to promote good public relations, especially mutual trust, between the 'Local Constabulary' and community, I was in the habit of putting on a civilian jacket over my uniform and visiting local 'Public Houses' late in the evening, which I found most productive as far as information regarding local criminal activity was concerned. During many visits to 'The Green Tree', I got to know a local workman, named Sydney, who had a large family. He often gave me information 'over a pint' which on occasions even concerned the activities of his own family. Sydney found it difficult to survive financially and in view of this situation he and his wife took in a rather tall and handsome male lodger.

Circa 1965, just before Christmas, Sydney returned home one evening to find that his wife 'had run away with the lodger' leaving no food or presents in the house for Christmas. I spread the word around the local 'Business Community' and it was not long before Sydney was inundated with both ample food supplies and toys etc for the children. Sydney was very grateful to all concerned and asked me how he could repay the community for their kindness. I immediately told him that he would have to remain at home with his family from the day before Christmas Eve until the day after New Year's Eve and to ensure that he did so one of my Constables would regularly visit the household throughout the period to check the situation. Under the circumstances, both Sydney and his children experienced a happy Christmas period. During the middle of the following January, Gwen and I were in bed when at about 0130 the front door bell of our Police

House rang. As usual we ignored it, knowing full well that if anyone wanted to contact me in an emergency they would use the telephone. After the caller was unable to rouse me by ringing the bell, he started throwing grit up at the bedroom window. This became intolerable. On opening the window, I saw a local wealthy fishmonger, who also owned a large house on the main road between Wallingford and Cholsey, kneeling on the lawn together with another figure whom I later found to be Sydney. The Fishmonger stated, "A little while ago I was awakened at home by Sydney who told me that he had just followed his lodger, who had earlier returned home with Sydney's wife, from Wallingford towards Cholsey and then stabbed him to death. I saw that Sydney was greatly distressed and covered in blood so I have brought him to you." I took them to the Police Station, statements were taken and later Sydney was duly charged with 'Attempted Murder', the lodger having been rescued from the scene with his life intact. On appearing at The Berkshire Assizes, Sydney pleaded guilty. The Judge called me into the Witness Box to further outline the circumstances of the offence. When I had completed my report, the Judge turned to Sydney and asked him if he agreed with my statement of the circumstances. To my great surprise Sydney replied, "I know Sergeant Dick Allen very well and we have often met up for a pint at the local Pub. Whatever he says will be right and I have great faith in him." The Judge was rather taken aback by this reply which resulted in jocular comments from him. Sydney did not go to prison, receiving what would be considered today as a 'suspended sentence'. To my knowledge, Sydney never fell by the wayside again and his marriage continued without any great problem.

During a very hot summer Sunday afternoon circa 1965 I was called to an incident of 'Alleged Indecent Exposure' to an eight-year-old girl on the river bank. I later duly arrested the male accused, charged him with the offence and bailed him to appear at the Didcot Magistrates' Court. At about 0930 on the day of the hearing just as I was leaving Wallingford for the court appearance at Didcot, I received an unusual call from my Divisional Commander, Superintendent Headley Phillips as follows: "I have just received a telephone call from Buckingham Palace to the effect that the Duke of Edinburgh's 'Personal Pilot' on Queen's Flight at RAF Benson is appearing in front of the Didcot Magistrates' Court to answer a charge of 'Indecent Exposure' and that you are apparently involved. Why is it I have only just heard about the arrest?" Reply: "As far as I was concerned it was a routine arrest and such a call was not necessary under the circumstances prevailing at the time". Evidence was duly given by the 'Prosecution' and the Defendant was strongly defended. Owing to the fact that the eight-year-old witness 'did not come up to scratch with her evidence', the Magistrates dismissed the case. On leaving the court for the car park, I then witnessed a rather attractive lady go up to the defendant and embrace him 'in a most loving manner'. I was then told that she was overjoyed by the result of the hearing, especially as they were getting married the following day. About a month later I was meeting one of my constables at a 'Conference Point' outside the Wallingford Post Office when a car abruptly stopped in front of me containing the former defendant and his newly acquired bride. He said, "Good morning, Sergeant, I hope all is well you. I have just returned to duty from my honeymoon, and you will be very pleased to hear that I have just been promoted from Squadron leader to Wing Commander." He then drove off and I never heard any more about the matter.

Whilst stationed at Wallingford, we resided in a very pleasant modern detached house in its own grounds not far from the Police Station, which adjoined a semi-detached house usually occupied by a Constable. Circa1965/1966 I received information from my Force Headquarters that the Force had held a 'Recruiting Drive' in Durham and that one of the applicants had been successful and would be moving into the detached house with his wife and very young son. Time went by and I heard nothing further about this matter until about 0230 hours one morning I was awakened by the said constable and informed that he had just arrived with his family. Owing to the hour we had no alternative but to accept the family into our residence until a reasonable hour arrived. To say the least, problems ensued before long and they did not prove to be' very good neighbours'. During a late afternoon in April, I was looking out towards the main Reading Road when I saw the Constable (with no helmet and his tunic completely unbuttoned) chasing a man up the Reading Road towards the Town Centre. Later enquiries revealed that the man was an 'Irish labourer' (Didcot Power Station was being built at the time mainly with 'Irish Labour') whom the Constable had found hiding within his home having an affair with the Constable's wife. The couple then separated, leaving the Constable residing in the house, and his wife and son moving in with a local 'Bachelor GP' and becoming his 'Housekeeper'. During the evening on a 'Maundy Thursday' I was on duty in the Police Station when the 'Bachelor GP' called at the Police Station to report that he had been cut across the back of his neck from ear to ear by his housekeeper with a razor blade but although the injury was quite apparent he did not wish to make any complaint and certainly would not support any proceedings owing to the scandalous gossip which would arise as the result. He then left the police station. The following morning I received a telephone call from the landlord of the Rowbarge Public House stating that there was a fire at the Bachelor GP's flat and the Fire Brigade were in attendance. I immediately attended the scene and found that the fire had been deliberately started by the Housekeeper. I arrested the Housekeeper and conveyed her to the Police Station where she was duly charged. During the period she was detained at the Police Station she reported that she was pregnant and needed medical attention. A Duty Doctor was called and after examining her (on the Police Station Counter') he came to the conclusion there was nothing wrong with her and that she was certainly not pregnant. In due course she appeared at Didcot Magistrates' Court where she pleaded guilty to 'Arson' and was placed on 'Probation' for two years. A few weeks later it was found that she was not complying with the Probation Order and was duly later sentenced to two years' imprisonment in Holloway Prison. On the day she was released from prison, she again appeared on my doorstep pleading poverty. I gave her her railway fare back to Durham (out of my own pocket) and I never heard anything further from the woman. The Constable was moved and served his 30 years with the Berkshire Constabulary without promotion.

It should be noted that owing to the excellent relationship we had at Wallingford with the 'local Press' during my period there, nothing whatsoever got published regarding these incidents.

Wallingford Section, being situated adjacent to the River Thames, was frequently involved in recovering human bodies from the river, which often caused problems as to whether Oxfordshire or Berkshire should deal with the problem. This inevitably resulted in much activity from

the Police point of view by jumping into the river, propelling the
bodies from one side of the river to the other. As far as Wallingford
were concerned, inmates of the local Fairmile Mental Hospital, Cholsey
were in the habit of regularly ending their lives.

Unfortunately, there were many accidents on the river resulting in
fatality. One particular case immediately comes to mind when the
owner of a very smart river cruiser was sitting in a deck chair on top of
his boat, reading, when the bough of a tree on the river bank plucked
him from his seat and threw him in to the river. We were immediately
called to the scene but could not locate him. Next day the Berkshire
Constabulary Underwater Search Team found him, unfortunately
deceased, standing on the riverbed upright, holding on to the bank
underwater with his spectacles still in place. The other passengers
aboard below decks had not realised there had been an accident until
the boat went out of control and hit the bank, too late to assist the
deceased.

In August 1967 I received promotion to the rank of Inspector in charge
of the Woodley Sub-Division and was very surprised during my last
evening at Wallingford to be picked up and taken to the Crown Public
House, South Moreton, where my Inspector, Tony Jones, had secretly
arranged a farewell party for me with many present.

In conclusion, I must mention that during my period at Wallingford I
became the first officer in the Berkshire Constabulary to be investigated
under the 'Complaints against the Police Act, 1964'. A complaint had
been made against me regarding my arresting teenagers at their home
at Cholsey at 0400 hours in the morning for thefts in the area the

previous evening. They were later charged and convicted of the thefts. The investigation was carried out in depth by Superintendent Roland Sparks who was at the time Divisional Commander of the Newbury Division. I was later fully exonerated. Little did I know that at that time I would in later years on reaching the ranks Superintendent and Chief Superintendent spend numerous hours investigating such complaints myself.

WOODLEY

After serving six years in the rank of Sergeant with three postings, my family found themselves uprooted from a very pleasant four-bedroom house in its own grounds at Wallingford to a comparatively small detached house in the grounds of Woodley Police Station on my promotion to Inspector and my posting to Inspector in Charge of Woodley Sub-Division. To start with the house was situated adjacent to the A4 Trunk Road from London to Bath which meant that on many occasions officers at the Police Station had to stop all the traffic on the A4, almost every time any of my family, or for that matter any police vehicle, wished to enter the A4 in a motor vehicle (M4 not in existence then).

The house was also vulnerable as we found out when it was burgled just after midnight one night when we were all in bed. On a dark winter's evening in 1967 a great baker friend of mine called at Woodley Police Station and asked me if his house could be placed on the attention list that night as he would be attending the Annual Dinner of the Bakers Association in Reading of which he was the President. Apparently his house had been burgled on a number of occasions in the past when the event was taking place. His absence was duly recorded and his house visited.

On this particular evening my wife and I retired to bed at about 2300 hours. Just after midnight I heard noises apparently coming from the actual Police Station. I picked up the phone and told the staff to keep quiet as our sleep was being disturbed. The Station Duty Officer replied, "Sorry, Sir, we are not guilty but you may like to know we have just arrested a burglar trying to break into the front of your house. As you are the victims, I have called the Chief Inspector out at Wokingham to take over the case." The Chief Inspector, complete with CLD, Scenes of Crime and Arc Lamps duly arrived on the scene with great haste The attendance was 'way over the top' making it possible for motorists passing on the A4 to consider that 'something was going on'. At about 0130 hours the said 'Baker Friend' arrived home to find his house intact and decided to call at the Police Station and thank the officers personally. You can imagine the comments that were passed when he found that my house had been broken into. The Housebreaker was a Vagrant on the road and did not realise that he had chosen a Police House to break into. He duly received a short period of imprisonment which he was pleased to accept because it was a shelter for a time.

As time progressed at Woodley I found the Sub-Division to be very busy 24/7 for both myself and the three shift sergeants – dealing with serious crime and serious road traffic accidents, many of which sadly proved to be fatal. I was also extremely busy prosecuting cases in the Reading County Magistrates Courts and the Juvenile Courts which proved to be of no great burden for me as I had acted as Court Officer at Ascot and Bracknell for some years.

In January 1968, however, all this valuable experience came to an abrupt end with the sudden death of the Deputy Chief Constable of Berkshire, namely Richard Baker, who had held the post for many years. At this time the whole force was looking forward to amalgamation with four other forces, namely Buckinghamshire, Oxfordshire, Reading Borough and Oxford City on 1st April 1968. Our Chief Constable had been nominated as the first Chief Constable of the Thames Valley Constabulary (renamed Thames Valley Police two years later) with the Chief Constable of Oxfordshire as his Deputy.

In January 1968 all forces concerned with the 'Amalgamation' were arranging to close down but Berkshire was faced with a problem owing to the death of the Deputy Chief Constable. A further problem was the fact that all forces concerned had seconded certain Senior Officers to Kidlington to assist with the formation of the new force. As far as Berkshire was concerned the heads of all Departments, with the exception of Administration which in this case was represented by the Deputy of the department, were seconded to Kidlington, Oxfordshire HQ, having been chosen as the new Headquarters. The Berkshire Superintendent, Administration was delegated to take over the Chief Constable's duties in Berkshire and I was seconded from Woodley to Sulhamstead to assist him.

Until the close down of the Force on 31st March 1968, the Superintendent and I were busily involved in closing everything down as a Force Headquarters ready for the building to be transferred to a

Force Training Centre and in fact both attended the last 'Standing Joint Committee' meeting to report the task had been completed.

Towards the end of March 1968 I was informed that I would be promoted to the rank of Chief Inspector on 1st April 1968 and appointed the Chief Inspector in charge of Administration on the newly formed Bracknell Division which included the new Sub-Divisions of Windsor and Wokingham.

BRACKNELL DIVISION

On 1st April 1968 I commenced my duties as Chief Inspector in Charge of Divisional Administration, Bracknell Division, taking over all 'Administrative Measures' to include inspection of all Force Owned Housing and Maintenance of same and responsible for 'Mass Catering' when required at short notice for such as 'Broadmoor Escapes' and other major incidents.

The situation of not being 'operational 24/7' as on previous two postings allowed me more time with my family and greater opportunity to involve myself more with voluntary projects within Bracknell New Town. Having been a Rotarian in Wallingford I was quickly invited to become a very active member of the Bracknell Rotary Club, which in turn enabled me to be included on a rota as a Voluntary Driver of early 1952 ambulances for the local Red Cross Detachment and eventually a Co-Chairman of the annual Bracknell Show with the Round Table Chairman. Shortly afterwards my wife began her 50-year stint with the Inner Wheel.

On Amalgamation the Bracknell Division inherited two very thriving Social Clubs at both Bracknell and Windsor Police Stations, which created a great family atmosphere for all serving and retired members and their families and ensure such annual events as Christmas Parties for all including children of all ages, Police Balls and many other social activities which no longer exist today. A good Bar and Dining Facilities were also available, especially at Windsor Police Station.

As Rotarians we enjoyed a very close arrangement with the RAF Staff College, Bracknell, inviting two 'Overseas Students' to dine with us at weekly meetings. This resulted in the Rotary Club being invited regularly to dine at the College. Members of the Division and their families were also invited in those days to enjoy various entertainers visiting RMA Sandhurst.

Whilst at Bracknell my daughter Louise became the sixth member of the family to be educated at Ranelagh School, Bracknell, which at the time was the only Church Grammar School in the Diocese of Oxford and it was for that reason I declined a move to Force Headquarters in 1970. In 1972, however, the Force was reduced from six Divisions to four, which entailed the closing down of the Bracknell and Witney Divisions. As a result of this situation I was appointed 2 i/c of the Force Inspection Team which had a Force-wide responsibility but allowed me to remain in a Force Rented Bracknell Development Corporation four bedroom house on the Wild Ridings Estate in Bracknell.

Later in the summer of 1973, whilst attending a Southampton University Management Course in a Hotel in the New Forest, I received a telephone call from my Chief Constable that he was promoting me to the rank of Superintendent with appointment of Commandant of the Force Training Centre at Sulhamstead and Training Officer for the Force. The family then moved in to a very acceptable four-bedroom house in its own grounds at Sulhamstead.

Whilst at Bracknell I had purchased a second hand 16-foot towing caravan which had to be stored in the winter at a relative's house in Crowthorne. The move meant no more problems with parking/storage of the van which enabled extensive holiday touring whilst residing at Sulhamstead.

RECOLLECTIONS OF A PAST MEMBER
OF ROTARY INTERNATIONAL

On joining Rotary International, many Rotarians do not fully appreciate the implications or the responsibilities undertaken and the risks taken when embarking on voluntary work with the community. My following recollections will no doubt illustrate the point.

Circa 1970 the Rotary Club of Bracknell was approached by Mrs Betty Kingdom of The Red Cross to supply drivers for an organised day trip to Bognor on a Saturday for Senior Citizens in the Bracknell area. I duly volunteered and on the morning of the event was allocated an old 1952 Bedford Ambulance complete with 'Bell' which had been converted to seat about a dozen passengers, one of whom was seated on my nearside. At approximately 0900 hours I started picking up my passengers, some of whom were confined to wheelchairs. Having picked up all my passengers, I headed along the A322 towards Bagshot en route to Bognor. On reaching the junction of the A322 with the A332 just north of Bagshot, it was necessary to join the A332. Vision to my left on the A332 was somewhat limited and not helped by the fact that I had an aged gentleman seated in the seat adjoining the driving seat. I asked the gentleman if all was clear to the left and on being informed that it was, I edged forward on to the A332 at a slow speed (acceleration on 1952 Bedford Ambulances was very poor especially when heavily loaded), and continued on towards Bagshot. Having travelled about five miles, a Land Rover drew up alongside me and the driver informed me in rather vulgar language that I had been responsible for putting a heavy goods vehicle heavily loaded with pipes off the road whilst joining the A332. The Land Rover then drove on and I pulled into the side of the road. Having been advised by my passengers that they had not witnessed any incident since leaving Bracknell and having formed the opinion that a return to the scene by me would (a) indicate a possible guilty conscience and (b) delay the trip to Bognor, I decided to travel on to Bognor. On arrival at Bognor, I was still somewhat concerned about the alleged incident at Bagshot and approached a Senior Member of the Red Cross who was also a member of the Bracknell Rotary Club, namely Rotarian Bertie Melhuish, on the matter. His reply was: "Don't worry at all about it, Dick, the Red Cross is fully insured against every eventuality." Having received such assurance, I decided to enjoy the day at Bognor. The day continued relatively peacefully although one 'Senior Citizen' in a wheelchair caused a few problems by stating that she was not enjoying the day as much as she had done with the British Legion in Bognor the previous week and remonstrated with the helper pushing her chair to the effect that he was (a) not going fast enough and (b) not going in the direction she wanted to. The 'Senior Citizen' continued to whinge to such an extent that eventually the relationship between helper and wheelchair passenger deteriorated to such an extent that the helper applied the brake to the wheelchair and left her on her own, waving her arms about, until another helper took over.

At about 1800 hours the ambulance was again loaded and we began the journey back to Bracknell. Singing commenced and all went well until we were approaching Chichester when suddenly one lady on board suffered a heart attack. I pulled up the ambulance and whilst attending to the lady sent another passenger to phone for an actual ambulance.

Within a short period the Sussex County Ambulance Service arrived on the scene and took over the casualty. There was, however, another problem in that I, under the prevailing circumstances, was considered 'next of kin' to the sick patient and as such would have to accompany her to St. Richard's Hospital, Chichester. I pointed out to the Ambulance Service that I had another 11 passengers to convey back to Bracknell. The Ambulance Service replied, "Well you will have to take your ambulance and your passengers with you to the Hospital and wait there until they have informed the 'next of kin' and you are released. I did as I was told and we all sat in the Accident and Emergency Department at St. Richard's for about 1½ hours until I was released. The remainder of the journey went without incident although we were one passenger short.

On eventually arriving home about 2215 hours, I got my own car out and returned to the junction of the A322/A332, Bagshot. There I was faced with the scene of numerous broken pipes scattered all along the grass on the south side of the A332 about 200 yards from the junction with the A322. There was no sign of an HGV vehicle, but commencing about 300 yards from the junction were heavy skid marks. It immediately appeared that the HGV had been travelling at a very fast speed and that the driver had been unable to control his vehicle when seeing a slow moving vehicle ahead.

On reporting for duty on the Monday morning I decided to inform Chief Superintendent John Snowley of the events of the previous Saturday. He listened intently to my story but passed no comment on same. Nothing further was said until about the Thursday when I received a 'Notice of Intended Prosecution' for dangerous and careless driving of a 1952 Bedford Ambulance signed by a Chief Inspector colleague of mine who held the appointment of Chief Inspector, Prosecutions for the Division. I duly approached John Snowley on the matter and he rendered a lecture on 'Road safety' for about ten minutes and then burst out laughing and admitted that he, duly supported by the Chief Inspector, Prosecutions, Douglas Gordon and the Detective Chief Inspector CID, Peter EAST (both close friends of mine), had decided that as I had been so concerned about the matter they should make me the subject of a 'practical joke'. We all had a good laugh and that was the end of the matter, but I must admit it taught me a lesson what could happen when involved in voluntary help. Nothing was ever heard from either the firm owning the lorry or the driver. I am pleased to say that the lady fully recovered from the heart attack and sent a very thoughtful letter of thanks to the Rotary Club of Bracknell.

THAMES VALLEY POLICE FORCE TRAINING CENTRE

Whilst with the Force Inspection Team, and with no previous experience in 'Training', in 1973, whilst attending a Management Course organised by Southampton University taking place in a hotel in the New Forest, I was very surprised to receive a telephone call from my Chief Constable, David Holdsworth promoting me to the rank of Superintendent, and wishing me to take over the appointment of Force Training Officer Commandant of The Force Training Centre at Sulhamstead House. I accepted the position with alacrity, which I thoroughly enjoyed until being posted to Slough as Deputy Divisional Commander some 18 months later.

On arriving at Sulhamstead, I immediately found that I was taking over the post with the full support of a most efficient staff, led by a very experienced Deputy who was later promoted Superintendent Commandant in my stead, followed by an appointment to the 'Directing Staff' at Bramshill Police College.

At the time of arrival there were some 26 courses in existence, ranging from courses for Divisional Commanders, courses to prepare Inspectors for the Inspectors'' course at Bramshill, to refresher courses for Sergeants and Constables.

Whilst in charge at Sulhamstead, fully supported by my staff, I was able to introduce a number of new factors, e.g. Television training, production of 'Training videos', new techniques with the aid of the latest equipment, and the introduction of a number of influential speakers outside the Police Service to speak to the various courses on a variety of topics.

Through my outside contacts I was able to arrange for a representative of the then Southern Television to train the existing staff in Television Training without financial cost to the Force, and likewise I arranged for visiting speakers to give their services, the only costs being incurred were a Traffic Patrol Crew conveying the speaker from and to Reading Railway Station, plus a meal from the Training Centre Canteen.

The visitors were actually waited on in my office by my secretary, dressed as a waitress and a male cleaner dressed as a butler (both outfits having been obtained from a local charity shop).

Once a year all Divisional Commanders and Headquarters Chief Superintendents were required to attend a five-day residential course at Sulhamstead. On two of the days, all day visits were arranged to Heathrow Aiprort and the Royal Military Academy, Sandhurst, which proved to be a great success; the only financial cost to the Force being the petrol in the Training Establishment's 20-seater Bedford Duple coach.

During my period in command, I arranged for the then Director of Public Prosecutions, Leading Prosecution Counsel, Leading Defence Counsel, the Secretary of the Council for Civil Liberties, The Editor of The Times and many other distinguished persons. They would address the course on their chosen subjects, which would be followed by a long question and answer period. It was strongly felt by the senior officers on the 'Senior Officers Annual Course' and the 'Visiting Speakers' that these visits greatly enhanced the liaison between police and public figures and the police and Civilian Aviation Authority and Royal Military Academy, Sandhurst.

In addition to pre-mentioned courses, there was also a 'Police Cadet Training Wing' supervised by an Inspector assisted by a Constable (who had originally been trained by the Army Physical Training Corps, Aldershot whilst serving in the Corps of Royal Military Police as a PTI) to assist with the physical side of the training, which included 'Outward Bound' Courses, the Devizes to Westminster Canoe Race, Long Mynd Hike and the Dartmoor Treks.

Once a year a 'Cadet Passing Out Parade' took place at Sulhamstead complete with the Thames Valley Police Band and, whilst I was in command, visiting VIPs to take the salute and address the students included the Bishop of Oxford and The Commandant of the WRNS, Burghfield.

There was also a very active 'Sports and Social' Club in existence at the Training Centre which included a regularly opened 'Bar' and many other social activities throughout the year. The building was suitable for 'Large Formal Dinners' and during my period there I arranged for the Rotary Clubs of Caversham, Bracknell and Wallingford to convey disabled persons of all ages to view a number of Police Demonstrations and also afterwards dine at the centre. Later when I became The Divisional Commander of the Traffic Division and President of the Headquarters Officers Mess, I arranged for the Duke of Kent to be our

'Visiting VIP Guest' at a Dinner at Sulhamstead, which proved to be a great success.

My brief posting to Sulhamstead was entirely unexpected and proved to be most valuable and interesting, standing me in good stead for further advancement.

HMS Dauntless, Burghfield – Women's Royal Naval Service Initial Training Centre

The Thames Valley Police Training Centre was only about three miles North-West of HMS Dauntless. Intakes for Initial Training at Burghfield were once a month and therefore Passing Out Parades also took place once a month.

Early in 1974 the then Chief Constable David HOLDSWORTH (who had seen service as a Commissioned Officer in the Devon Regiment) was invited by Superintendent Viola McBride, WRNS Commandant of HMS Dauntless to be the VIP Guest Inspecting Officer at the next Passing Out Parade. He readily accepted the invitation and on the day called at Sulhamstead to change into formal uniform immediately before the event. He of course was in possession of a large Jaguar motor car with a uniformed chauffeur as befitted his rank. Apparently, the Chief Constable experienced a very enjoyable day in the presence of all the ladies.

Shortly after the event, I was informed by the Chief Constable that he had invited Superintendent McBride to be the Guest Inspecting

Officer at the TVP Cadets Annual Parade at Sulhamstead. The Annual Parade consisted of all the Cadets, Directing Staff at Sulhamstead and the Thames Valley Police Band with all parents and many other guests invited as spectators. Superintendent McBride carried out her duties in a magnificent manner and very much enjoyed meeting many present after the parade.

About a week after the Parade at Sulhamstead, the Chief Constable rang me to say that I had been invited by Superintendent McBride to carry out the duties of VIP Guest Inspecting Officer at a Passing Out Parade at Burghfield one month after HRH Princess Anne.

Although I readily accepted, I immediately considered there could be problems. The main one being what vehicle did I use to transport me to Burghfield for such a prestigious event? Our transport at Sulhamstead consisted of a 20-seater Bedford Duple Coach, a Mini-bus and an old Land Rover. I called to my office Sergeant Ray SAMPSON, a very experienced police officer and Instructor who had held a Commission in the British Army. He immediately came to attention in front of my desk and said, "No problem, Sir – I will deal with it, leave it to me to drive you over to Burghfield myself." The day came and I dressed in my best uniform, carrying my 'Swagger Stick'. Sergeant Sampson arrived at the front door of Sulhamstead House, complete with our old Land Rover which was completely unrecognizable. Polished, tyres painted, seats attended to – in fact, it looked as though it had just come out of a 'Car Show Room'. Sergeant Sampson was immaculate in his best uniform wearing a new cap with a 'slashed peak'.

When we arrived at Burghfield we were greeted first by a very smart Wren on guard who saluted me and then asked me in a formal manner for my 'Sword and Medals' to place in safekeeping. I, of course, had none. Superintendent McBride then intervened and took over the situation. After a very warm welcome she said to me, "Superintendent, you realise that HMS Dauntless is a female ship and the only males we have here are the Padre and the Boiler Man. We therefore have no male facilities so I will take you to my toilet and stand on guard outside the door whilst you are in there." This procedure was carried out and I was then given details by the Superintendent of what would be required of me as Inspecting Officer etc. namely, firstly, after the Wrens were in 'Open Order' on the parade ground she would escort me to the parade and introduce me. She would then accompany me through the ranks whilst I inspected all the Wrens and spoke to a number of them during the process. After this I would mount the rostrum and take the salute as the parade passed me by. After the parade the whole parade would retire to the Gymnasium where I would address them for some 45 minutes regarding their future. When the Parade had been dismissed, I would be taken to the Ward Room where all 'Officer Ranks' would be present.

All went well with the parade and talk, and on arrival at the Ward Room with the Superintendent I encountered three very attractive WREN Officers stood in line to welcome me. The first said, "Your cap, Sir" and took my cap. The second said, "Your gloves, sir" and took my gloves. The third said, "Stand in front of the door, Sir" and stood in front of the toilet door until I came out. There then followed an hour of drinking accompanied by delightful conversation. At the end of the hour it was announced that we would all then adjourn to the

Commandant's Private Bungalow for a five-course meal accompanied by wines depending on the course and then an excellent selection of liqueurs etc. The meal was eaten and much wine etcetera consumed. Some hours later Sergeant Sampson was called and took me safely home to my official residence. A day that neither Ray nor myself would ever forget.

Several weeks later I received a telephone call from Viola stating that she had been invited to the TVP HQ Officers Mess, Kidlington as a VIP Guest and would I like a lift as she noticed I only had an old Land Rover at my disposal. I readily accepted the lift. On the day of the event a black Limo, complete with a Royal Ensign flying from the radiator, pulled up outside my official residence at Sulhamstead. Out got Wren Bird from the driving seat before walking to my front door, saluting and escorting me to the rear offside door of the vehicle. I got into the back seat and found a most radiant WRNS Officer formally attired in the WRNS Officers Mess 'Mess Dress' complete with all its badges of rank etc. She was beautifully 'made up' and her perfume was exquisite. She moved towards me and gave me a very warm welcome and we both entered into conversation until arriving at HQ Kidlington where we found the members of the Mess lined up outside main entrance to greet us. Viola alighted from the vehicle first and I followed. If you could have only seen the shock in all the members' faces when I came in with her! We were then escorted to the Bar for pre-dinner drinks prior to the Banquet. I was of course seated with Viola throughout the evening. We arrived back at Sulhamstead safe and sound about 0100 after a thoroughly enjoyable and memorable evening.

As the dark nights of winter approached in 1974, I received another call from the Chief Constable informing me that the Regional Women's Police First Aid Competition would be held at HMS Dauntless over a coming weekend and would I visit on occasions during the weekend and ensure all was going well?

About 1900 hours on the Friday night I again visited HMS Dauntless as instructed. I was greeted by the WRNS Duty Officer who said, "I will show you round and then I have been instructed by Superintendent McBride that I am to take you to her bungalow for dinner. I arrived at the bungalow and again received a very warm welcome from Viola. Apart from staff attending upon us, we were left on our own for a lovely evening of pre-dinner drinks, wines at the table, an excellent meal and liqueurs for the rest of the evening which finished about 2245 hours. We shook hands and wished each other all the best for the future. Later Viola received another posting and progressed further in the ranks and I was posted to Slough and in due course also received further promotion.

PETER IMBERT LATER LORD IMBERT

Peter IMBERT was the fifth of seven children of William, a Kent farmer. He attended Harvey Grammar School in Folkestone and worked in New Romney Town Hall before 'National Service' with the Royal Air Force Police. After 'National Service' he joined the Metropolitan Police in which he eventually became the Deputy Operational Chief of the Anti-Terrorist Squad when he achieved the 'highest profile of his whole career' being the Chief Negotiator during the Balcombe Street Siege when four IRA members were holed in with two hostages in a flat in Central London in 1975 for six days, which ended peacefully mainly through his negotiating skills. It was shortly after this incident that I first met Peter when he and his colleagues were invited by the Slough members of CID for a social evening in the then very active 'Slough Police Social Club'. Amongst the party invited was Peter's Commander (Commander Jim NEVILL whom I had previously met and who became a friend of both Gwen and myself and with whom we attended a number of social events in London. He was not at all smitten with Imbert and it is unfortunate that IMBERT took most of the credit for the outcome of the event. Whilst IMBERT 'basked in glory', NEVILL was very much in the background being a person of very modest personality.) At the time I was in fact the Deputy Divisional Commander of the Slough Division, Thames Valley Police, which covered the Sub-Divisions of Slough, Windsor, Maidenhead and Bracknell with a total staff of 1,200. At that time I found Peter to be a very affable, charming and modest person who was nevertheless proud of his achievement and ambitious for the future.

In 1975 Peter was promoted in the Metropolitan Police to Chief Superintendent (a rank he only held for two weeks) before achieving the posts of Assistant Chief Constable and later Deputy Chief Constable of Surrey.

In September 1975 I commenced Part 1 of the Senior Command four-month course at Bramshill Police College. Whilst I had been a guest at 'Guest Night' at the College on two occasions previously, I had not been to the College before, mainly owing to the fact that I had only held the rank of Inspector for seven months. During my period at Bramshill, Peter and his wife Iris attended the Guest Night on a number of occasions when I met his wife and Peter met Gwen.

I was not very enthusiastic regarding attending the course in the first place mainly because I was thoroughly enjoying the experience of policing at the 'Sharpe End' of the Thames Valley Police. As a result I did not settle down well to college life, especially as far as socialising in the bar was concerned and during syndicate periods. After about six weeks had elapsed my Syndicate Instructor (a lovely Chief Superintendent from the Met who was due for retirement after my course) hauled me up in front of him in private and advised me that he was very disappointed with my progress, mainly because of my lack of social attendance at the Bar and lack of contribution to 'Syndicate Discussion'. He further stated that the College had been in contact with my Chief Constable over the problem, who had stated that I was behaving 'completely out of character' as far as Thames Valley was concerned. It was later learned that this call from the College was first received by Inspector Peter WINSHIP, David HOLDSWORTH'S Staff Officer at the time who eventually became Sir Peter WINSHIP, HM

Government's Inspector of Constabulary. Shortly after this incident I received a personal call from David HOLDSWORTH informing me that he had not been impressed by the way that Peter WINSHIP had dealt with the call and was forwarding his personal apologies over the matter, having suitably advised Peter WINSHIP on his actions. The Syndicate Director stated that as a result of the conversation with the Chief Constable, l would be appointed 'Social Secretary' for the course with a view to bringing me back to character.

I then arranged a social programme for the period covering the remainder of the course which included a private whole day visit for the course to Pinewood Film Studios complete with guided tour of the studios and lunch (all at no cost) followed by a visit to the Slough Police Club in the evening, a day visit to Portsmouth mainly for a guided tour of HMS Eskimo by the Captain and the final dinner (5-course banquet with all wines etc. for the total of £10 per head) at the Officers Mess of the Army Catering Corps Training Establishment at Aldershot. At the conclusion of the dinner I was approached by the Commandant of the Centre and asked if I would nominate four Senior Police Officers, one each from Kent, Surrey, Hampshire and Thames Valley forces who could be invited to become Honorary Members of the Officers Mess. As a result of the conversation, Peter Imbert (then ACC in Surrey), the Divisional Commander of Aldershot Division, a Senior Officer from Kent and myself were also invited, which resulted in the four and their wives enjoying excellent evenings as guests of the Mess for some years.

Towards the end of the course my vvife Gwen stated she would very much like to invite three members of the course, who could not regularly travel home owing to the distance involved, to come over to our house at Slough for Sunday lunch. She requested, however, that she would like their arrival delayed until 12.30pm in order to be able to prepare the lunch. As a result two members of the Royal Ulster Constabulary and one from Strathclyde were invited. Knowing that they would prefer to leave the college at about 1000 I decided to arrange for them to attend The Chapel at Royal Lodge, Windsor Great Park for Morning Service. I met them on arrival at a 'Gate' at the Park at 1030 and guided them via Rangers Gate to Royal Lodge. On meeting up at the Gate I advised what would probably be happening and that possibly members of the Royal Family may be in attendance and further instructed them on procedures accordingly. On being seated at the rear of the Chapel it became apparent that the Queen, The Duke of Edinburgh and several other members would be present. On conclusion of the service I was approached by an Equerry that Her Majesty wished to speak to my guests and requested that they meet her on approaching the Main Drive. l was advised to keep my distance as HM was already aware of my presence and position. Her Majesty engaged all three in very interesting conversation for 15 minutes. The four guests then carried on to Slough where they enjoyed a good lunch, a short nap and interesting afternoon at Slough. On arrival at Bramshill the following morning I was greeted by many requests both from Directing Staff and students for lunch at Slough with the same experience before the end of the course.

After the course my Chief Constable received a very favourable report on my progress from Bramshill. In January 1977 I received information from the then Deputy Chief Constable, Leonard DOLBY, that I had been earmarked for promotion to Chief Superintendent in command of the

Reading Division when the present incumbent retired who at that time was well within the bracket of retirement. For me, unfortunately, he did not retire for a year or so afterwards and I was duly promoted and granted the post of Chief Superintendent, Traffic Division / Deputy to the Assistant Chief Constable, Operations based at HQ Kidlington with effect from 1st May 1977.

Whilst serving at Slough I carried out the duties of Divisional Commander for one year whilst the Divisional Commander was seconded from the Force as President of the Superintendent Association travelling the UK. Towards the end of my time at Slough I was also greatly involved with the preparations for the Silver Jubilee, especially in the Windsor area, and as a result Gwen and I were invited to attend the Royal Enclosure, Windsor Great Park, when HM lit the first bonfire in the country.

Life on the Slough Division for a Commander and his Deputy was very demanding and resulted in an average of a 90-hour week. Eleven days and nights on the trot with a Friday, Saturday and Sunday as Rest Days every other weekend. You were 'on call' 24 hours via telephone, pager or the 'Force Radio' you were compelled to have fitted in your private car (mobile phones were not in common use in those days). If you were called, you immediately realised the reason for the call would be to require your immediate decision/attendance. This situation regularly interrupted your 'family life' thus causing disappointments for the family.

Slough Division was required to deal with the highest crime rate in the Thames Valley Police area and frequently involved the most

serious crimes and often the issue of firearms. I served at Slough
from November 1974 to April 1977 and during that period no one day
passed without a Police officer being injured on duty somewhere in
the Division. The IRA were frequently active within the area and I
personally took command of five sieges (all with a successful outcome
during the period).

Circa 1976 I was called out during one evening to a number of IRA
incidents in Farnham Road, Slough, a very busy main road adjacent
to the very large Slough Trading Estate, Slough, mainly consisting of
bombs being placed under motor vehicles. On arrival I found Captain
GOAD, RAOC Bomb Disposal and his team in attendance. During
my period at Bracknell as a Chief Inspector (1968-1972) we lived in a
rented 'Executive Type' house in Pickering, Wild Ridings, Bracknell,
and Captain GOAD had been a near neighbour whom I passed the
time of day with most days. I then accompanied the team for about
two hours and at about 2140 Capt. Goad informed me that he would
have to leave the scene as he had been called to an IRA bomb incident
in Kensington, London. We shook hands and exchanged best wishes.
Later on I retired to bed in our house in Kendrick Road, Slough and as
I was off duty later the same day I remained in bed until lunchtime.
On going downstairs I found the television news on and was very
shocked to hear that Captain Goad had been blown up at the scene
at Kensington, receiving instant fatal injuries. A memory that still
haunts me today!

During my period at Slough I found myself taking command regularly
at IRA and other 'Terrorist Incidents'. At one stage when the Prime
Minister of the time ordered tanks to surround the whole of the

Heathrow Airport perimeter, I was placed in command of the TVP Contingent who were dealing with our side of the Surrey/Berkshire border. Intelligence had suggested that Terrorists were going to blow up a 747 aircraft shortly after take-off in the vicinity of the Staines Reservoir.

Throughout my career in the Police Service it was always very necessary to maintain a good relationship with the National and Local Press. On our arrival at Slough my Divisional Commander was of the strong opinion that we should invite members of the 'Local Press' into the Slough Police Club for a social evening in order to further cement relations. The evening appeared to go well. A few months later the Divisional Commander decided to recommend a local resident in Slough for a Thames Valley Police Award. His recommendation was granted and the Divisional Commander duly arranged for the presentation to be made by the Slough Corporation at one of their meetings when the Press would be present. Unfortunately the recipient did not arrive at the designated time of presentation, as a result of which the Slough Sub-Divisional Commander was requested to send a patrol to the recipient's address to ascertain the reason for his non-appearance. This, however, proved unnecessary as at the time the recipient was in police custody in the cells at Slough. The situation was duly reported by a very embarrassed Divisional Commander to the meeting. On receipt of the next edition of the Slough Observer newspaper, the main headlines on the paper read 'RED BLUSHES UNDER THE BLUE LAMP' with a full explanation of the situation recorded below for all to read. The headlines caused great concern to the Divisional Commander, especially considering the recent social gathering at the Slough Police Club. He called me in to his office and instructed that in future I was in charge of all press relations as he no longer wished to communicate with them.

TRAFFIC DIVISION

In 1980 having been the Divisional Commander of the Traffic Division, having carried out successfully two periods as Acting Assistant Chief Constable, Operations, and also attended a three-day interview at Eastbourne for selection for Part II of the Senior Command Course, I found that on return from Eastbourne Leonard Soper my by then Acting Chief Constable (later Chief Constable of Gloucestershire) had been informed that I had only just missed selection and would be seconded to the Police College Directing Staff the following Tuesday to 'knock off some rough edges'. Apparently a Lady on the Selection Board was concerned over my 'West Berkshire' dialect. I refused the offer and remained with Thames Valley Police Headquarters, the rest being history.

Also in 1980, Peter Imbert was appointed Chief Constable of Thames Valley Police. Our relationship continued well, and Gwen and I were invited to his house and again met Iris. We also invited him and his wife to various functions of the Oxford North Rotary Club in order that he may meet local personalities. It was quite apparent, however, that whilst he was well read, very approachable and charming in his manner, his experience outside the Metropolitan Police in general and Special Branch and CID in particular was very limited despite his short periods as ACC and DCC with the Surrey Constabulary, a situation which he clearly understood and being very ambitious for the future was very willing to rectify. The general first impressions of his Divisional Commanders at the beginning of his reign was that he had been promoted at the time beyond his capabilities having only held the rank of Chief Superintendent for two weeks and that experience in another force as a Divisional Commander would have granted him much needed experience before further advancement. It must be stated that the 'rank and file' of the Thames Valley Police, outside of Force Headquarters, were quite impressed with their new Chief Constable, mainly because of his approachability and charm, and remained so until he eventually left in 1984 to take up the position of Deputy Commissioner to Commissioner Newman, Metropolitan Police.

Peter Imbert immediately got very involved with the whole of the Force and all its responsibilities, working long hours seven days a week (frequently in his office until 2300 hours even on a Sunday), together with the social side of the Force. At the time of his arrival there were at least ten very active and prosperous 'Police Social and Recreational Clubs', which were not only supported by regular police and civilian staff, but also by their families and pensioners together with the HQ Officers Mess and The Southern Area Officers Mess (I was first Founding Secretary of the Southern Area Mess for about 18 months and later President of the HQ Mess Committee from 1977 to 1980).

Peter Imbert became an enthusiastic member of the HQ Mess (complete with 'Mess Kit' at £350 per set) and greatly enjoyed getting to know all the members and guests. At one guest night, held at Kidlington, Superintendent Ivan Forder, Commander of the Aylesbury Sub-Division, brought along as a guest the Private Secretary to The Duke of Kent, a Commander Royal Navy Rtd., who was brought up originally in Sandhurst Road, Crowthorne. As my paternal grandmother had rented a house and raised a family, including my late father, in High Street, Crowthorne, until 1945, I was well aware of the area and in consequence knew many residents past and present, including a builder who had built a bungalow in the grounds of Wellington College for the said Commander's mother. When l was introduced to the Commander, we found immediately that we had a common interest and a conversation developed which very soon led to us addressing each other by our first names. Peter Imbert, who had been watching the situation carefully, came to the wrong conclusion that we were in fact old friends, a matter I denied. He then said to me, "Go and ask him if there is any possibility that the Duke would be willing to accept an invitation to our next Guest Night" which happened to be at Sulhamstead. At first I objected to carrying out the request, but the Chief Constable insisted that I did. On explaining my embarrassment to the Commander, the Commander appeared very receptive to the request and suggested I ring him in person the following Monday morning and gave me his telephone number. I rang the Commander as suggested and was informed that the Duke of Kent would be very pleased to receive such an invitation. The event was held, a large number of VIP guests also in attendance, and all members of the Mess were presented to the Duke with the exception of my good self who was granted a private audience with the Duke at his request. When Chief Superintendent David Peterson's turn came along, he was asked by the Duke if they had ever met before to which he replied, "Yes, your Grace. When you were about five and riding your tricycle around 'Coppins' you nearly knocked me over when I was on duty there." Immediate laughter all round. The evening proved to be a great success and remains a very memorable occasion.

On another occasion Peter Imbert approached me and asked me how well I knew The Duke of Marlborough and stated that he was aware that the Duke's Agent, Administrator and Farm Manager were all members of the Oxford North Rotary Club. He then requested that I should ascertain whether the Duke would accept an invitation to attend a Mess Night, this time to be held at Windsor Police Station. I duly made the necessary approach to those mentioned above and received a reply back to the affirmative but with the rider that the Duke would be travelling to the event from his London residence and not Blenheim Palace. On the morning of the event, the Chief Constable instructed me to travel to Windsor during the morning/ early afternoon and on return to HQ confirm to him in person that all necessary arrangements were in place. I considered this journey completely unnecessary as I had already confirmed the fact with the Superintendent in charge of the Windsor Sub-Division, but I still had to go and report back. On going to the Chief Constable's Office I also found the Chief Superintendent, Operations was visiting. At this time both the Chief Superintendent, Operations (a great friend of mine throughout Berkshire and TVP) and myself were both of the strong opinion that enough experience had been gained at HQ and it was time to get back to a more interesting task, that of being a Divisional Commander of a Territorial Division and we were both well aware that a vacancy was coming up at Oxford. On the spur of the moment, whilst waiting to be seen by the Chief, we decided it would be a good opportunity to put the case together to the Chief and 'test the water'. This resulted in an amazing and memorable reply, i.e. 'That he had a new Chief Superintendent, namely Wyn Jones in charge of the Newbury Division who had very recently transferred to the force from Gloucestershire as a stepping stone and was destined, on instructions from 'On High' to be Divisional Commander of Oxford Division then Assistant Chief Constable, TVP, followed with high rank within the Metropolitan Police'. (And looking back in the past that is what exactly transpired.) On return from Windsor I confirmed all was well at Windsor, the only minor change being to the seating plan. The Chief Constable's attitude changed instantly and a stupid exchange of opinions resulted in my being informed that he was not stupid but in a fact a long-standing member of MENSA. As a result of this situation I very quickly came to the conclusion that deep down he was completely devoid of a sense of humour and things were the never same between us afterwards. (Please see Chapter on Freemasonry for actual reason, which did not come to light until his 'Obituary' in The Guardian Newspaper after his death.) That evening The Duke delayed the whole proceedings for one hour, by arriving late at Windsor, and Peter Imbert got into a situation where at the last minute he realised that he had invited a Peer (Ex Senior Police Officer) as well as a 'Duke' and did not quite know how to deal with the situation. The end result was that I was seated next to the Duke of Marlborough and The Peer of the Realm was with the Chief Constable. When the Chief got up to welcome the guests to my (and everyone else's) amazement he announced that 'we have here with us this evening His Grace the Duke of Marlborough who is the personal guest of Chief Superintendent Allen and if that is not one-upmanship I do not know what is'. The Duke and I were amazed as the Duke thought he was the Chief Constable's guest. He, however, took it very well, thoroughly enjoyed the evening until about 0200 hours and sent me a lovely letter of thanks afterwards, which I still possess. We had many interesting guests on that occasion including Terry Wogan (later Sir Terry Wogan) whom I had met first whilst I was at Slough.

On one occasion Peter Imbert called me to his office and stated that he had received a request from the Oxford City Bus Company to present the 'Annual Road Safety Awards' to their successful drivers and that he had hoped to carry out the task himself particularly as he was proud of the fact that his father was in fact a London Transport Bus Driver, plus the request had included him being allowed to drive a new double decker bus, in uniform, through the streets of Oxford for publicity purposes. He saw no problem with this as it was legal to drive such a vehicle with an ordinary driving licence provided that no passengers were on board. He regretted, however, he was committed on the proposed date of the event and therefore unable to carry out the task, and was therefore instructing me to take his place. I replied to the effect that I would carry out the presentation but declined to drive a very large, expensive new vehicle as requested despite the fact that I had had experience of driving vehicles of up to seven tons in weight in the Royal Military Police. I duly carried out the presentation and did agree to drive their old double decker bus, used for training, around the bus depot yard. The following year the Chief Constable received the same request again and on this occasion drove a new Oxford Bus Company Double Decker (in full uniform) around the streets of the city, complete with the full attention of the media thus appearing on television etc. Later in the year whilst all the staff (served by the Senior Officers) were in the 'HQ Canteen' thoroughly enjoying their annual Christmas meal, their meal was suddenly interrupted by an 'Urgent PA Announcement' as follows:

"Would Driver Imbert please report to the garage as a matter of urgency as his bus is still awaiting him."

Imbert went balmy and immediately ordered a full enquiry into the matter, thus again illustrating his complete lack of a sense of humour on occasions.

On another occasion I was instructed to accompany Peter Imbert and his driver in his official Jaguar to a Funeral Service in Devizes for one of the Wiltshire Constabulary Constables who had been tragically murdered. At the time we should have departed from Kidlington, the driver and I were sat in the car but still no sign of the Chief Constable who was well noted for being a poor time keeper. About an hour later he arrived on the scene and immediately ordered me to put my cap on which was nigh impossible being in the back seat of the vehicle. I complied, however, which meant that my knees were half-way up the back of the driver's seat for the whole journey. Speed limits were ignored and just as we arrived at Devizes the coffin was about to be carried through the main door of the church. The driver and I were immediately ordered to follow the Chief Constable closely. As the coffin was approaching the actual door, we went up the side of the coffin, cut in front of it, entered the church and went straight to our reserved seats in front of the whole congregation – an extremely embarrassing situation. Later in the day I switched the television on at home for the news and was then horrified to view the whole disgusting debacle. All we should have done in the circumstances was to wait discreetly until the coffin was in the church and then sit at the back!

In an 'Obituary' published in the Guardian newspaper, it was stated that one of the greatest achievements of Lord Imbert was the permission granted to Roger GRAFF of the BBC to make a 'Fly on the Wall Documentary' within the Thames Valley Police. This view is certainly not that of a number of senior officers serving in the Force at the time, including myself, who made our views on such a proposition known at the time. The 'Documentary' was made and later shown on television creating a great deal of discussion both inside and outside the force. I will content myself with just two matters in which I was personally involved, i.e. my refusal of a number of requests from Roger Graff at very short notice to avail himself of transportation by Traffic Division vehicles already engaged on patrol to convey him from one side of the force to the other. Despite my refusal, Graff contacted the Chief Constable in person on every occasion and my decision was always overturned, without consultation for reasons, no matter what problems were caused. The other occasion concerns the filming of a 'Promotion Board Interview' of a candidate for the post of 'Chief Inspector' on which I was required to sit in judgement. On arriving at the interview, I found cameras and other BBC equipment installed and on questioning the matter I was informed by the Chief Constable that not only the interview would be recorded in full but also the private discussion held on the candidate's suitability afterwards. I immediately registered my objections to both aspects. The Chief Constable over-ruled both objections by stating that the candidate had, not surprisingly under the circumstances, agreed to the situation. The candidate failed to be selected for promotion and many months later I was horrified to view both aspects of the interview fully shown on BBC Television. I knew the candidate well and to my knowledge despite being worthy of promotion was never promoted further during my time in the Force.

Chief Superintendent Jones progressed to Divisional Commander of Oxford Division as planned and to say the least we did not see 'eye to eye' on a number of occasions, mainly because he possessed the modern academic theory held by 'Bramshill Police College' at the time which was duly engrained into the new 'Fast Track Regime' that Traffic Divisions should either be greatly reduced in strength or abolished all together. l will not here, take up many pages supporting the valuable input by 'Traffic' e.g. protection of property, detection of crime and number of arrests resulting etc achieved by the members outside their 'Traffic Responsibilities'. Every member of the Traffic Division had to prove that they had a first-class record in 'General Police Duties' before they were even considered for the Traffic Division. Wyn Jones also possessed unusual ideas regarding persons arrested in that he had been known to release prisoners arrested on the authority of his Deputy from the cells without discussion with the Deputy. Shortly after one incident the Deputy Commander involved, a first class Senior Officer, became my Deputy. He had to wait until my successor retired before further promotion to the post of Commander, Traffic Division. Shortly after this episode, Chief Superintend Jones was promoted to the rank of Assistant Chief Constable, Operations and became our boss. Anyone who did not know Jones well would get the impression of a very smart, well groomed senior officer who was very articulate very well read, right on top of his job, well experienced and well able to command any major incident at short notice. To start with he would appear very helpful and friendly. Later you quickly get the impression that this personality only comes to light to those who work for him directly on a daily basis and submit and agree with everything he does or says and when he wishes to make the impression to further his promotion prospects. He was always very hostile to anyone who dared to question his instructions or views leading him to appear to be uninterested in alternative views, completely unable to have any respect for the feelings and situations of his subordinates and extremely self-centred. To describe him as a 'Bully' at times would not be overstating the matter. After a short period it was quite obvious to me and other Senior Officers stationed at Kidlington that Peter Imbert was petrified of Jones, mainly because if he did not please him in every way he too would not achieve his goal of being Deputy Commissioner and later Commissioner of the Metropolitan Police. Whenever Jones overruled my orders to my Division regarding day-to-day traffic matters without any consultation with me whatsoever, the Chief Constable without any hesitation would always support Jones without even listening to my reasons.

During the Summer of 1982 relations between Jones and myself continued to deteriorate and on one Friday in the October I was behind my desk at Headquarters when I received a telephone call from a long-standing colleague/friend, namely Superintendent Joseph Benham, Sub-Divisional Commander of the Aylesbury Division. We had served together in Berkshire through the ranks and like me he had served his 'National Service' in the Corps of Royal Military Police. He said, "I would just like to chat about the change-over next Monday." He immediately came to the conclusion there was a problem and said, "I take it you are fully aware that I have been promoted and appointed to your position as from Monday and you are going to take over the Banbury Division same day."

I was shocked and devastated to say the least and had been given no notice at all about the change. I immediately went to the Chief in his office and protested vehemently about the whole situation. He would not look me in the face and after appearing very shaken he said, "Has not Mr Jones put you in the picture?" I replied in the negative, left his office and returned to my department and duly put my HQ Staff in the picture. Without exception, they were all amazed/shocked and very sympathetic. I left work early that Friday as arrangements for me to be picked up by ACC Harry Ross at home and conveyed to an event in Slough with the Thames Valley Police Band (Ross was Chairman of the Band Committee and I held the post of Secretary) had already been finalised. For me the evening proved to be a complete disaster and best forgotten. Next morning, a Saturday when I should be on a weekend off, I travelled to my office at Kidlington 'to clear my desk'. Shortly after my arrival I was called by the Chief into his office and for almost an hour l lambasted him with my feelings regarding him and Jones and the disgusting manner in which I had been dealt with. He just sat there, let me carry on and made no effort whatsoever to stop me.

In the end he just said, "Dick, there is only one difference between me and you. If you had passed the extended interview at Eastbourne and I had failed, you would now be sitting in this chair and I would have been standing in front of you." I was so shocked with the manner in which he had demeaned both himself and his rank that I left his office and went home without further comment.

Being posted to Banbury meant that I had a round trip of 50 miles to travel each day as opposed to the round journey to Kidlington of 24 miles which amounted to double the actual cost and double the time taken. Being Commander of the Banbury Division was no challenge whatsoever for me, having previously had the experience of being Divisional Commander of the Slough Division. I was bored stiff throughout the two years I held the post and found it very difficult to occupy myself for eight hours a day when on duty. I was never called out, but I did experience a problem with shortage of staff during the 'Miners' Strike in the North of England' circa 1983 when I was ordered by the Chief Constable to suspend all patrols in rural areas and to adopt 'Fire Brigade Type Policing' in the towns. The Chief Constable rarely visited me or even spoke to me. I did meet him on the occasion of HM Inspector of Constabulary's Inspection of the Division which apparently went very well, but the Chief never spoke to me about the result.

ACC Jones did visit me on a number of occasions owing to the fact that the CND were very active with their demonstrations at USAF Upper Heyford at the time. Before my arrival he had apparently pestered my predecessor regarding two 'Celebratory Cutlasses' on which were plaques endorsed 'Presented to the Oxfordshire Constabulary' apparently presented for some reason many years previously, which were on view in the Chief Superintendent's suite of offices at Banbury. I had not been at Banbury long before ACC Jones again started pursuing possession of these antiques. On two occasions I refused his request, stating that the objects would not leave Banbury as far as I was concerned. On the third occasion he literally ordered me as my superior to agree to his request. I again resisted but he still persisted in a bullying manner. As a result I called in my Secretary at the time and instructed her to contact the Divisional Administration Sergeant at the time and instruct him to report to my office at once with the 'Station Inventory' on which was recorded the two cutlasses. ACC Jones duly signed receipt on the inventory and took away the cutlasses. Later the same morning I was in my office when a WPC (whose name I cannot recall) came into my office and said to me, "Look out of the window,

Sir, and see what is going on in the outside yard." I immediately did as requested and there saw that ACC Jones and his driver had loaded his car with a quantity of antique books etc (possibly Occurrence/ Crime registers etc.) and were in the process of leaving the yard. I immediately came to the conclusion that ACC Jones was removing further antiques without any permission. The question instantly went through my mind was should I intervene immediately, seize cutlasses and other property and contact TVP Headquarters without delay. I immediately realised that owing to the past/present relationship with myself, the Chief Constable and ACC JONES, I would probably not receive any support whatsoever with the problem, particularly bearing in mind that both had great expectations of promotion in the Metropolitan Police in the near future. I decided in view of the circumstances, that despite what the Divisional personnel may have thought of my lack of action, to turn a 'blind eye' to the occurrence. A decision I have greatly regretted ever since. I was later informed that a large antique clock had disappeared from Chipping Norton Police Station possibly under the same circumstances.

CND demonstrations were a common problem and 'Operations' regarding same were usually organised by Headquarters, Operations Department with inputs from Division when necessary. At the time the Thames Valley Police Band was very much in existence with regular practice periods and outside public engagements which undoubtedly aided 'Police/Public Relations'. ACC Ross was the Chairman and I had been Secretary for some years. During one of the CND demonstrations, with the Chief Superintendent, Operations in Charge on the ground, the Annual General Meeting of the Band was held at Sulhamstead being a central point in the Force and I was duly required to attend

as Secretary. The meeting was arranged to start at 3.00pm and about
4.00pm the meeting was interrupted by an urgent call from ACC
Operations in person. He immediately wished to know why l was
at Sulhamstead, a long distance from my Division. I explained the
situation, which was not accepted, and he immediately ordered me to
return to his office at Headquarters as a matter of urgency to be briefed
by him regarding taking over command at Upper Heyford. l returned
at great speed to Kidlington as instructed, only to be informed by his
secretary that he had gone home and left no instructions for me. I then
proceeded to Upper Heyford where I met the Chief Superintendent,
Operations, who was intending to spend the night on the operation.
He could not understand what was going on and we decided we should
remain together on site for the night. At about 0830 the next morning,
Jones arrived on scene and asked why l was there. I then explained the
situation to which he replied with a smirk/grin, "There was no need
for you to be here all night –resume your duties on Division."

In August 1984 the Chief Superintendent, Operations retired and to
mark the occasion ACC Jones acquired an aeroplane complete with Pilot
and flew his HQ Staff to Le Touquet for a day trip to commemorate the
occasion. Shortly after this occasion he transferred to the Metropolitan
on promotion to the rank of Assistant Commissioner. JONES at the age
of 40 years was widely regarded as a future Commissioner, but circa
1993/1994 following a 'Misconduct Enquiry' HM The Queen withdrew
his 'Warrant', he having been previously found 'Guilty' of 10 of the
original 31 allegations investigated.

Peter Imbert soldiered on until early in 1985 when he too returned
to the Metropolitan Police with promotion to the rank of Deputy

Commissioner, later he became Commissioner. Our paths briefly crossed afterwards first at a District Rotary Conference held at Eastbourne in March 1985 when he was the 'Speaker' and on two occasions much later when he and his wife were guests at an Oxford Club. On the latter two occasions he did not appear very keen to communicate with me but his wife Iris greeted my wife and I with 'open arms' and long conversations with her revealed she was finding his retirement very difficult to cope with because she was constantly acting as his Secretary and Driver owing to the fact that he appeared totally unable to use 'Public Transport' and carry out such tasks himself. Sadly he was later struck down with constant ill-health and reduced to a wheelchair. He passed away in 2017.

I retired at the end of 1984 and after six months' unemployment carried out the duties of a 'Positive Vetting Investigating Officer' employed by the Ministry of Defence and attached to the Royal Air Force and Security Service for just over ten years, which involved extensive travel both home and abroad. Having again signed the 'Official Secrets Act' on retirement from this position, I am unable to comment further. I can state, however, that in this post I was a Civil Servant with the rank of Higher Executive Officer coupled with the Honorary rank of Squadron Leader.

Since retirement I have often wondered what may be recorded on my personal file especially as there have been a number of incidents since, e.g.:

1. Whilst carrying out my duties as Manager of the Paddock for the Ascot Racecourse Authority circa 1996, I was approached by

the then Assistant Chief Constable Operations, Thames Valley Police, namely Ian Blair, later Commissioner of Metropolitan Police, in full uniform (it was well known at the time that HM The Queen was certainly not in favour of 'uniform' on the course) who said, "Hello Dick, how are you?" I replied, "I have never met you" to which he replied, "I know you well by reputation". We then discussed a problem regarding the division of responsibilities between the Police and the members of my staff.

2. Circa 1995 I applied to be considered for the advertised post of a 'Non Executive Director' of an Oxford-based NHS Trust as I considered I had gained sufficient experience for the task when I was with the Thames Valley Police Inspection Team 1972-1973. After a number of successful interviews for the post I was placed in a 'Pool' to await consideration when a vacancy arose. Circa 1996 as I had heard nothing further, I wrote a letter to the then Secretary of State for Health, Dr Liam FOX, who replied with a very long detailed letter which basically stated I was of the wrong 'Political Colour' to be finally selected. Shortly after receipt of this letter I was approached by a fellow member of the Kidlington and District Probus Club at a monthly meeting and threatened with action if I did not 'Keep my nose out of the NHS' and stuck to 'Security Matters'. The fellow member was believed to be a Retired Local Government Officer who is now residing with his second wife in Somerset – a Doctor/Former Senior Administrative Member of an Oxford NHS Trust.

THE HORSE RACING INDUSTRY

Having arrived at East Ilsley during December 1931 at the age of three months, it was another two years before I began to realise as a very small child exactly where my parents had landed me. On looking back my first recollections go to being pushed by my father, accompanied by my mother, through the entrance gates into Newbury Racecourse for a day's 'Racing'. As I grew older, I found that there were 'Race Horses' all over the place which necessitated a strong warning that whenever a citizen of the village encountered any of these giant creatures they should immediately stop in their tracks until the very expensive animals had passed by in complete safety. Throughout my 16 years' residence in the village, the entire community strictly adhered to this warning, realising of course that the Horse Racing Industry employed a vast number and was also a necessary advantage to the local economy.

Ilsley's greatest claim to fame was back in the eighteenth and nineteenth centuries for Sheep Fairs and Horse Racing. Regular Sheep Markets, at first held weekly and then fortnightly, started in 1620 when Sir Francis MOORE, born in Market Ilsley, obtained a Charter from King James I to hold Markets every Wednesday from February to August. With the exception of Smithfield Market, Ilsley held the largest Sheep Markets in England. Up to 80,000 sheep passed through the Fairs in one day, mainly coming long distances using the Ridgeway. The last Fair was held in 1934, but pens were still in existence all round the village when I left in 1948.

Horse Racing in East Ilsley goes back to the eighteenth century when the Duke of Cumberland, brother of George II, had a large mansion called 'Kate's Gore' at the foot of the North side of Gore Hill with stables built there. The famous horse 'Eclipse', whom the 'Eclipse Stakes' is named after at Sandown, was born at the stables in 1764. The Duke of Cumberland also created a Racecourse nearby at Prestan Down where annual meetings were held until 1800.

At the time I was residing in the village there were four Training Establishments actually in the village and another four in close proximity. All these Trainers were treated with great respect and lived like Lords to whom everyone touched their cap. Residents in the village referred to them as either Mr or Sir, and children were expected to lift their caps if wearing one when passing them. I well recall such Trainers as EAST, LOWE, BLETSOE, GILBERT, TODD, GOOCH, STEADALL, CUNDELL, BEEBY and WAUGH and Jockeys such as BEASLEY, SMIRKE, GRAVES, FREDDY FOX (tragically killed on his motorcycle in a road accident on the A34 road bends near the Horse and Jockey Public House, Chilton circa 1937) and of course Sir Gordon Richards (who found it necessary to travel to Switzerland every winter for treatment for Tuberculosis).

Stable lads, many from Southern Ireland, at the time were housed in local Hostels and in fact some actually slept above their horses in the stables. Stable lads were poorly paid and endeavoured to supplement their income by giving out 'Tips' in one of the six 'Public Houses' which by the time I left the village in 1948 had been reduced to four, namely The Star, The Swan, The Sun, and The Crown and Horns. Both the Swan and the Crown and Horns had experienced great tragedies over their many years of existence with the suicide of landlords who had previously been involved with Horse Racing.

It was not unusual to meet a Stable Lad in a smart new suit showing off his new Morris Minor car after a huge win on the horses one week and meeting up with the same lad a few weeks later penniless.

I well remember my mother being in possession of a local newspaper photograph taken circa 1933 at Jack Waugh's stable at Chilton on the occasion of a 'Donkey Derby' showing my father entirely dressed in sacking and carrying large bunches of carrots in front of the donkeys running towards the Winning Post. The front donkey was in fact being ridden by the Champion Jockey at the time, namely Steve Donaghue.

In 1914 James EAST was the first to breed, own and train a Royal Hunt Cup winner at Ascot, namely 'Lie in a Bed'. On that memorable day everyone in the village was invited to a meal in a huge Marquee erected in a meadow. The local Silver Band actually led the children to the tent. The Newbury Weekly newspaper reported that a 'Meat Tea' of majestic proportions was served to 400 adults, which was followed by speeches and dancing well into the evening. People were able to view the silver cup and Lie in a Bed was duly paraded in the marquee.

I well remember the day when 'Commissar', trained in the village by Johnson-Houghton, won the Stewards Cup at Goodwood circa 1947. With permission of the Trainer I patiently awaited the horse's return to the yard and then took a photograph of him, coming down the steps of the horse box, on my old 1923 116 Kodak camera and sold copies around the village for sixpence a time.

During the time I lived at East IIsley, horses were transported to race meetings mainly by the Blue Horsebox Company based at Hendred. These boxes consisted of a tractor and trailer, in other words an articulated vehicle. They were considered to be the latest, most luxurious vehicles of the type on the road at the time. Some Trainers did have their own vehicles and I remember that Cundell owned one, which was always driven by the same driver who was known and beloved as one of the great characters in the village at that time. On one occasion, my father, taking me of course, managed to obtain a lift with this character to Epsom Downs conveying a horse called 'Jack Tack'. Having enjoyed a day's racing, unfortunately we experienced very heavy rain on returning to the 'vehicle park' and managed to get soaked to the skin, as a result we had to strip off all our clothes on reaching the box and travel home naked with the horse.

On another occasion I received an offer for a day out at Windsor Race Course from a local Travelling Head Lad. After he had seen me safely through the gates he said, "I am not sure at this stage what time we will be leaving for home. The horse is running in the second race so do not be too far from the exit from the winning enclosure. If the horse wins, keep your eyes on me when I go to wash the horse down. At this stage if I have both my shirt sleeves rolled up we will be staying on but if I have both sleeves not rolled up at all, get back to the box as quick as you can." The horse won and we were well on our way home before the third race.

Betting in those days was considered illegal but local residents and of course the Horse Racing Fraternity still continued the practice. Bets were placed in sealed envelopes and delivered to the local Public House

Landlords. Once a week a Reading Bookmaker (Southampton Street) travelled to the village and collected the envelopes, also paying out the winning bets from the previous week.

Residents made sure that they were present during the Bookmakers' visit because he was in the habit of calling for 'drinks all round' in every Public House visited which were greatly appreciated even if you had not placed a bet.

My first visit to Royal Ascot Races was in circa 1945 when my father and I were taken to Ascot Races by Harry GRAVES, Landlord of the Crown and Horns, East Ilsley, former Jockey of some repute having ridden the winner of a number of significant races during the 1920s, in his luxury open top touring motor car. At the start of the journey we were warned that we would have to hide the car at a Public House in High Street, Bracknell owned by a Bookmaker friend of my father as the car was running on illegal petrol (strict petrol rationing at the time owing to the War) and continue the rest of the journey to Ascot by taxi. On arrival at Ascot, Harry leaving the car to be parked in the Jockeys Car Park, we then proceeded to the Jockeys entrance to the course. Harry had a pass for my father but there was a question regarding my admittance. To my surprise (I was approaching 6ft tall and 14 stone at the time) Harry informed the Steward on the gate that I was in fact his son. The bowler-hatted Steward looked at me in amazement but still allowed me in. The day proved most memorable and enjoyable and it was the first time I had seen the 'Three Card Trick' being openly played along the pavements and the many other activities, lawful and unlawful, being carried out outside the course. Inside the course one of the most striking things I came across was the 'Tipster' Monalulu in exotic native dress shouting the odds. Little did I know at that stage of my life that in 1952 I would be commencing a long association with Ascot, finally ending in 2005.

After completing my National Service and initial Police Training at the Sandgate Police District Training Centre with the Berkshire Constabulary, I found myself posted to Ascot where I was allocated accommodation in the Single Man's Mess in which I stayed until my marriage to Gwen in December 1955. After marriage I continued to serve at Ascot until being moved to Bracknell in 1957.

In 1946 King George VI gave authority for three further meetings, i.e. in July, September and October, to be held in addition to the Royal Meeting. In 1952 the Ascot Racecourse only employed a permanent workforce throughout the year of about 50, headed by Sir John Crocker BULTEEL who resided in a purpose-built mansion on site with virtually three Departments, i.e. Administration, Grounds including the course, and Buildings. Douglas BUTT (Former Senior NCO in the Guards), was in charge of Administration, which included the 'Hiring and Firing' of Race Day Employees and the overall management of same. When HM the Queen was in attendance he also carried out the Duties of Comptroller of the Royal Box. When away from the Racecourse he was frequently hired by many local organisations as a Master of Ceremonies/Toastmaster, duly possessing the necessary official qualifications for the post. Over the years Douglas became a very close friend and remained so until he retired in 1980.

There was also a purpose-built Magistrates Courthouse on site for use during the Race Meeting which was used throughout the rest of the year once a fortnight by The Windsor County Magistrates.

On arrival at Ascot I quickly settled down and as far as the Racecourse was concerned the following took place:

1.   During the Race Meetings personnel actually serving at Ascot were required to carry out either 0600 hours to 1000 hours and later in the day 1800 to 2200 hours duty each day, or 2200 to 0700 at night. The local Police Officers were able to obtain 'Complimentary Tickets' for Tattersalls, which enabled us to attend the races if we so wished when we were off-duty.

No Annual Leave was allowed during a Race week and no member of the Force was allowed to attend any type of course. Some 500 personnel were drafted in from other Forces and those who could not travel daily were housed in a large Barracks which had been built for the Metropolitan Police before the Second World War. There were two Police Clubs available during the meeting, one on site at the Police Barracks and one at the Ascot Police Station. During Race Meetings, members of the BBC Camera Crews were regularly invited into the Club at the actual Police Station, and many enjoyable evenings were held with them.

Being a single man, and one of the few drivers qualified to drive all the vehicles at Ascot and later occupying the position of Sub Divisional Clerk/Court Officer at Ascot, I was usually allocated the daytime shift. Being on the spot this usually resulted in me driving either the Austin one ton van, fitted with bench seats, or the Bedford People Carrier (with steering wheel gear change) after the end of racing to Oxford Prison, conveying prisoners who had been sentenced to imprisonment by the Windsor County Magistrates sitting after the last race. As a general rule, any Magistrates sitting at the conclusion of racing had previously been treated as VIP Guests during the afternoon by the Ascot Racecourse Authority, thus creating a rather convivial atmosphere during court proceedings afterwards. This situation appeared to continue for the journey to Oxford, when my fellow officers acting as escort had the prisoners 'singing their heads off' within ten minutes of leaving the course for the rest of the 40-mile journey to Oxford. This situation changed dramatically by the time we reached the approach to the prison.

2. One evening just after racing had ceased, we received a call from a large house in Devonshire Road, Ascot, which had been rented out for the week by the owner to a 'well-to-do family', from London, complete with their entire 'Domestic Staff', to the effect that the house had been burgled and very expensive items stolen. A number of us attended immediately but searched both house and grounds without result. After we had concluded our part of the operation and awaiting the CID to take over, we were approached by the Housekeeper and invited 'Downstairs' for refreshments. Unfortunately, however, we could not take up the offer immediately as one of our number was missing, which required an immediate search again. After about five minutes he was found sitting in an ornamental pond with water up to his shoulders, complete with his helmet still in position, with a fish perched on top of same. As he was soaked to the skin, we made his

apologies to the Housekeeper for his absence and then enjoyed the very tasty repast laid on for us.

During the period I was serving at Ascot and living in Single Quarters, I was accompanied by an average of eight single men, all of whom had recently completed their National Service. Exactly one mile up the road, Heatherwood Hospital existed together with a Nurses Hostel. This situation of course was of great interest to the single men, especially when they had in their possession complimentary tickets for Tattersalls Enclosure at the course. There was, of course, no problem in persuading a young attractive lady to accompany you to the 'Races'. On one occasion a number of us spent the afternoon together at the races, including a colleague who was in fact engaged to a young Irish lady in Ireland. This engaged lady, unfortunately for my colleague who was enjoying an afternoon with a nurse, was watching the BBC Television in Ireland when she suddenly saw her fiancé on the screen parading in the Paddock with another woman. Next day during the afternoon I was on duty when the said Irish lady arrived at Ascot Police Station, without prior notice, complete with large suitcase. They did marry, but he later died prematurely at the age of 43 years.

Ascot Racecourse has experienced a number of problems over the years with inclement weather which has resulted in the day's racing being abandoned. Back in circa 1955 mid-afternoon during the 'Royal' meeting, a thunderstorm developed and the course was struck by lightning which electrocuted a pregnant lady who was leaning against a fence at the side of the course.

Circa 1957, Gwen, my wife, was attending a minor meeting at the course in the Paddock with her father when they witnessed the death of Manny Mercer, a leading jockey at the time. The horse and jockey were passing through the Paddock to go to the start when it reared up, causing Manny to be thrown into the air and on the way to the ground catching the back of his head on a post. At the time of the incident I was on duty at Bracknell Police Station where I was immediately instructed to go to the Mortuary and assist my Sergeant to lay Manny out. On stripping him down we came across an old grey pullover, full of holes, which we later understood was considered to be the lucky pullover he always wore when racing.

Circa 1954 I and my colleagues were assisting with traffic control at Shepherd White's crossroads, Ascot at about 13.30 during a 'Royal' meeting when we came across a frustrated Sir Gordon Richards who was stationary in the traffic prior to riding in the 2.30pm race. We extricated him from this situation and quickly got him to the Jockeys Room in time. He thanked us most profusely and then told us that he was riding the probable winner, namely a horse called 'Will Win' in the first race. Later on, we watched the race with some disappointment because we could not see 'Will Win' amongst the runners at all. It came as a great surprise when the winner was eventually announced. Apparently, we did not see the horse because the horse was so far in the lead. It won at 8-1 which greatly enhanced our income at a much-needed time.

In April1961 I left Bracknell for Abingdon on promotion to Sergeant which was followed by another move to the Berkshire Constabulary Headquarters at Sulhamstead in December, 1962. At HQ I again came into contact with the Ascot Racecourse Authority as it was one of my responsibilities to produce the Police Operation Order for the 'Royal' meeting. This was quite a complex task because in those days officers were personally selected for Ascot and then personally selected for each of the many posts. We also carried out all the catering at Ascot for police personnel, supplied cooks, waiters etc. from our own staff and grew most of the vegetables required in the gardens at Sulhamstead.

In May 1964 I was moved again to take over the Wallingford Section before being promoted Inspector to take over the Woodley Sub-Division in August, 1967. Throughout the period since leaving Ascot we kept up our friendship with Douglas and Gwen continued to frequent the Royal Ascot Race Meeting, always taking one of her many friends with her for company.

My career carried on to include another period at Bracknell as a Chief Inspector, Thames Valley Police, in charge of Divisional Administration, 18 months as Deputy to the Commander of the Force Inspection Team, followed by a similar period of time as Thames Valley Police Training Officer/ Commandant of the Police Training Centre at Sulhamstead.

In 1974 I was appointed Deputy Divisional Commander of the Slough Division of the Thames Valley Police which covered the South East of Berkshire and included the towns of Slough, Maidenhead, Windsor, Bracknell, and Windsor Great Park and Ascot Racecourse. During this period I often found myself taking charge of police personnel at Ascot. On one occasion on a very wet and miserable day I was informed at about midday that HM the Queen would be attending the meeting after spending the previous night at Highclere Castle as the guest of Lord PORCHESTER, later to become the Earl of Carnarvon. I also understood that she would be travelling with Lord Porchester and would be arriving at 1350 hours. At about 1320 hours I returned to the Ascot Police Station to check that all was well. At about 1330 hours I returned to the vicinity of the main 'Royal Gates' to the Members Enclosure when, in the rain I saw a Metropolitan Police Royal Protection car up against closed 'Royal Gates' with no one in attendance. Behind this car was a very dirty large saloon car. As I approached the car, a male person dressed in a sports jacket and no hat opened the driving door of the saloon car and started remonstrating with me about the gates being closed, complaining that HM the Queen was in the car and had been held up for many minutes. He then informed, in no uncertain manner, that my 'head would roll' for this situation. I quickly realised I was talking to Lord Porchester, HM the Queen's Racing Manager. Eventually Douglas BUTT, Controller of the Royal Box, opened the gates and later wrongly sacked the two Corps of Commissioners who were due be on the gate from 1400 hours onwards. Just after the first race, HRH Princess Margaret was taken ill in the Royal Box and insisted on being taken home. When her car and chauffeur arrived at the said gates, surprisingly they were found to be shut again because no one had, from the Ascot Authority, been instructed to man them in the absence of the sacked two members of the Corps of Commissionaires.

Just after the fifth race I was positioned in the centre of the A329 ready to wave HM the Queen's car on to the A329 in the direction of Windsor Great Park. This car was quickly followed by Lord Porchester en route to Highclere. He abruptly stopped the car, wound down the front offside window and said to me, "All is forgiven, Superintendent. HM the Queen's horse won the last race."

In 1977 I was promoted to the rank of Chief Superintendent with the role of Divisional Commander of the Traffic Division and Deputy to the Assistant Chief Constable, Operations and moved to The Thames Valley Police Headquarters at Kidlington. Although I was not personally involved with Ascot as much, members of my Division were heavily active at every Ascot meeting. During my period in this role I was in fact required to hold the Acting Rank, for a period of six months on each occasion, of Assistant Chief Constable, Operations on two occasions. One of these occasions coincided with the Royal Ascot Race meeting and I found myself acting as 'Police Escort' to the Royal Procession on the first day of the meeting, together with the Chief Constable's driver PC FOX driving the Chief Constable's Jaguar car, from Windsor Great Park to the Golden Gates at Ascot Racecourse. We duly arrived at the starting point, placing the car in a position to lead the procession immediately in front of the horses pulling the Royal Carriage. The 'Procession' started with all on board and travelled through the Ascot Gate, up to Cheapside and along to the Golden Gates. At this point we left the procession to carry on up the course and we travelled via public roads to the Royal Enclosure, duly parking the car therein until the arrival of the procession. After the procession was completed and HM the Queen had entered the Royal Box, her Equerry of Horse, Col. Sir John MILLER, approached me with a horse whip in his right hand and reprimanded me for allowing the Jaguar Car to go too slowly, thus causing the exhaust fumes to enter the nostrils of the lead horses and cause them discomfort.

On another occasion early in the Royal Ascot Race meeting I received a telephone call from an Equerry at Buckingham Palace stating that HM The Queen was rather concerned about the unnecessary number of police motorcycles, and their position on the road, employed to escort her on her departure from the course to Windsor Castle via Windsor Great Park each day, pointing out that she did know the route very well and was not likely to get lost.

Up to this date the escort usually consisted of a Sergeant motorcyclist in front of the 'Royal Car' and four motorcyclists, two behind the Sergeant, one on the nearside and the other on the offside of the 'Royal Car' and two at the rear of the 'Royal Car' following the front two motorcyclists.

On receipt of this observation I gave instructions that the same number of motorcycles should be employed for 'Security reasons' (such as IRA still being active etc) but with the Sergeant far more in advance with the two motorcyclists so as to be almost out of the view of the Royal Car and the rear to drop back to a position where they were not readily noticed. On the first occasion this new formation was used the whole convoy set off down the High Street over Sunninghill crossroads, over the Cannon crossroads and then down to Blacknest Gate. At this point the escort realised the Royal Car was not following, causing great concern. The Sergeant duly reported the problem on the radio but after a short while a message was received that HM the Queen was safely back at Windsor Castle, having turned left at the Cannon crossroads and travelling to the Castle via Ascot Gate instead of Blacknest Gate.

Not very long after this incident the Sergeant involved retired and at his 'Farewell Presentation' I was handed a brilliant A4 size cartoon to present to him. The cartoon displayed the Sergeant on his motorcycle being chased by the Duke of Edinburgh on a polo pony waiving his polo stick and shouting to the Sergeant 'How dare you lose my wife'.

Just after the First World War a 'Titled Philanthropic Lady' resident in the Ascot Area was of the strong opinion that a Club should be formed for the enjoyment and welfare of members of the Armed Services who had served during the war. As a result of her wishes accommodation was found for the Club amongst the Ascot Racecourse buildings. This project went well until the Ascot Racecourse Authority gave the members of the Club notice to vacate the premises. This action so concerned Prince Edward, the Prince of Wales at the time, that he brought the notice of his great concern to his father, King George V. As a result of this intervention, the Ascot Racecourse Authority allotted a parcel of land on the South of the A329 road on which was built the Ascot Ex-service Men's Club, later becoming a very thriving business until the late 1990s. Sadly, after struggling for six years, the Club was forced to close in 2006. During its 'heyday' both Prince Edward and later Prince Charles were active members and it is well known that Winston Churchill also took a great interest in the progress of the Club. In 1952 I became a member of the Club for many years (later I was granted Life Membership as a result of my contribution to the Club), and thoroughly enjoyed its many activities. The most striking aspect of this Club was that you were able to take part in the activities on a level platform without any formal division of past rank and status.

In circa 1965 Sir Nicholas Beaumont was appointed Clerk of the Course at Ascot and shortly afterwards, whilst resident in Wallingford, I was summoned by the President of the Ascot Ex-service Men's Club at the time to attend a function at the Club, being held especially to welcome Sir Nicholas to his new post. It was requested that I introduce him to the members of the Club as I had previously served at Ascot and was still a respected member of the Club. From that day onwards until I retired from the 'Police Service', I was able to enjoy a very good professional relationship with Sir Nicholas, especially when I reached higher rank in the Thames Valley Police. Sadly, this relationship did not continue when I retired as you will read later.

I eventually retired from the Thames Valley Police in December 1984 and after a break of six months, during which I was Positively Vetted for my new career, I became a Positive Vetting Investigating Officer attached to the Provost and Security Service of the Royal Air Force with effect from May1985. During this period Gwen and I purchased an apartment situated in Rincon-de-la-Victoria, Malaga, Spain.

During our period in Spain circa 1990 a former police colleague of mine, who had also purchased a villa in Rincon, arranged a Thames Valley Police Pensioners Reunion at his villa. He and his wife put on a sumptuous meal and a variety of alcohol products. About 30 attended who either lived permanently in Spain or had purchased villas in the country.

When our host, a former Chief Superintendent, retired from TVP, he took up a part-time occupation with the Ascot Racecourse Authority as 'Race Day Manager of the Paddock'. (At this stage it must be explained that at this level at Ascot there were three Race Day Managers, namely one in charge of the Paddock, one in charge of the Royal/Members and a third in charge of Tattersals, Silver Ring, Boxes and Turnstiles.) At the reunion he stated that at the time he was experiencing a problem at Ascot in connection with IRA activities in that he had no female staff available to search ladies' handbags on their entrance to the course and asked for volunteers. About six ladies volunteered, including my wife Gwen. On returning to the United Kingdom they were all recruited, my wife was appointed their Supervisor, and their duties on the course commenced in 1990.

In 1991my wife persuaded me to apply for 'Gate Steward's Duties' at Ascot. I was accepted at the lowest level and given the task of protecting a piece of grass in the Paddock from the deposit of bottles, glasses etc. In 1992 I was duly promoted to guarding a gate from No. 1 Car Park into the Paddock. On my first day I was duly engaged in my duties when I was visited by the Clerk of the Course, Sir Nicholas Beaumont, who on approach said, "You are not doing your job, ALLEN. I have had complaints that you are allowing persons to gain entrance without paying by climbing over the wall." I pointed out that that was impossible as the wall adjacent and the arch over the gate had glass and other objects set in cement on the surface. He did not accept my answer and stamped off in indignation. At this stage I was amazed at the attitude the Clerk of the Course had adopted, especially as he knew me well in the days I was a Senior Officer in Thames Valley Police on first name terms when dealing with Ascot matters and the fact he had been talking absolute rubbish. Shortly afterwards I was visited by the Chief Security Officer at Ascot (a former Chief Superintendent I knew well) who asked me how I was getting on. I related the incident to him and he said "leave it with me I will deal". About half an hour later the Security Officer returned with a member of the Ground Staff who was pushing a wheelbarrow loaded with black treacle. To my amazement the workman started brushing black treacle all over the walls and the gate arch. On completion the Security Officer remarked, "That should do the trick", and left the scene.

Later the Clerk of the Course returned to the scene and remarked "What on ever has gone on here." I explained the action in full to which he replied, "I can understand that the yobs will be deterred but I don't think the better class punters will be too pleased when they get treacle all over their 'Ascot Clothes' when they climb over. I was again left in amazement until a couple of years later I was personally involved in an incident in the Paddock with Lady Beaumont.

In circa 1994 I was appointed Deputy Manager of the Paddock and a year later I took over the job as Manager. In circa 1993 I was on patrol with the Manager, a retired Detective Inspector from TVP, when we came across a man dressed in full top hat, tails etcetera carrying a black board displaying in chalk a number of quotations, sayings etc. Attached to his lapels were a very large number of metal badges and on the top of his top hat was strapped a 'Child's Toy Crane' which was whizzing round at a speed. It was quite obvious that he was trying to address the crowd with some controversial subject which was causing extreme annoyance. Such was his conduct we considered that he should be removed from the course onto the public highway (A329) which was running adjacent to the Paddock. This proved far more difficult than we anticipated and attracted the interest of the public. About an hour after his despatch from the course, we were called to the main Ascot Authority Office where we both duly reprimanded for our action. Apparently Lady Beaumont had seen the said person outside her dwelling and had duly given him a 'Complimentary Ticket' for Tattersalls.

The Paddock Manager and his staff were responsible for many duties e.g. dealing with a crowd that could reach a height of 40,000 at any one time, ensuring the safe passage of horses from the stables to the Paddock and on to the Starting Gate and back, manning 'Gates' etc. One of the most important and difficult tasks involved HM The Queen and HM The Queen Mother. Whenever either, or both, wished to visit the Paddock area or the stables situated therein, they would inform HM's Representative who would signal the Royal Box Controller (known as 'Black Top' on the radio), who would in turn inform the Paddock Manager by radio that a 'Perambulation' was about to take place. The Paddock Manager would then move towards the Royal Box accompanied by a female member of his staff. If HRH The Queen Mother (complete with Golf Buggy and Chauffeur) was attending as well, The Paddock Manager would accompany her (together with a female member of his staff), leaving The Deputy Manager to attend HM the Queen (also with a female member of the staff). No 'Operation Order' or previous instructions were in existence, which meant that HM Representative only had about two minutes' notice of any movement.

These very flexible arrangements led to many interesting incidents with both HRH The Queen and her Mother, but first I will deal with HRH The Queen Mother.

On the first day of the Royal Ascot Meeting circa 1996 HRH The Queen, on entering the Royal Box, approached my predecessor as Controller Royal Box/Royal Liaison Officer, namely Wing Commander (Rtd) JOHNSON and said, "I regret that I have another problem for you this year in that my Mother will be attending, complete with her Buggy and Chauffeur, and will be requiring attention when moving in the Paddock area." At the first available opportunity Johnny JOHNSON informed me of the conversation and said, "Over to you."

I together with my female member of the staff, a very tall, elegant, well-spoken lady, on receiving the radio signal from 'Black Top' duly met the Buggy (dressed in HRH The Queen Mother's Racing Colours) at the entrance to the Royal Enclosure. At this stage we found Lord and Lady Oswald positioned on either side of the Buggy and the Chauffeur in the driving seat with HRH The Queen Mother by his side. Fortunately for me I knew the Chauffeur well and was able to communicate with him in a relaxed manner.

Off we went towards the Paddock with HRH duly instructing the Chauffeur which led us straight into the crowd and up against a fence near the exit to No. 1 Car Park. At this stage a call was received from Black Top, who was escorting HRH The Queen to her stables: "Management is concerned as to the whereabouts of her Mother. She requests that you raise your radio above your head and as you are very tall she will no doubt be able to see you." This action was taken and I was duly thanked. On returning in the direction of the Royal Enclosure, HRH The Queen Mother frequently stopped and conversed with members of the public, particularly if she thought they were 'Housewives' on subjects ranging from cooking, cleaning, racing and many other topics. Bearing in mind it was always necessary to get HRH back to the Royal Box in time for the next race, these interventions were not helpful and usually ended up by the four of us accompanying the Buggy to break into a trot for the last 100 yards or so. Somehow one of those very welcome persons, as far as HRH was concerned, who always came across was Sir Peter O'Sullevan, retired Racing Commentator, which without fail always started a long conversation regarding the racing which proved difficult to bring to a conclusion.

On one occasion HRH The Queen Mother got herself in the centre of the Parade Ring on foot, leaving the buggy outside a very muddy circular track on which the horses paraded whilst awaiting the jockeys to mount. As HRH was wearing a lovely clean white pair of shoes, I instructed my staff to move the chauffeur and buggy to the inside of the track so as to ensure HRH could get in the buggy and keep her shoes clean. All my efforts to please HRH were in vain. She retorted: "Tell that man to put the buggy back where it was." Her order was carried out and as a result her tights and shoes were covered in thick mud. I must state that amongst all 'the trials and tribulations' we received whilst escorting HRH, Lord and Lady Oswald were always extremely helpful and considerate to both my staff and myself, which was greatly appreciated.

Throughout all HRH The Queen's perambulations she was extremely co-operative, but there were occasions when I and my staff did get it wrong as far as she was concerned. This situation was usually caused by the lack of staff numbers allocated to the Paddock by the Ascot Racecourse Race Authority.

On one occasion things did go very wrong all day particularly with the containment of bottles, glasses etcetera, which resulted in the rubbish getting everywhere, including across HRH's route to the Royal Box. This led to HRH frequently complaining about the situation all afternoon. During this sad period I was leading HRH and her representative back along the route to the Royal Box when I found a 'Drunken Punter' shouting obscene remarks in front of and within hearing of HM. I asked him to move but it was necessary for me to wave my radio at him in a threatening manner to achieve my aim. I said to him, "Stand to one side, HM The Queen is behind me." To which he replied, "Bugger the bloody Queen, I want the loo."   To my amazement I was told by a member of the Ascot Authority about an hour later that Her Majesty was not happy about the way I dealt with the drunk and that I should curb my actions.

On another occasion when I was in fact with my female member of staff, ensuring HM the Queen and her entourage's free passage through the Paddock and into the Parade Ring, HM stopped short of the horses' track because horses were approaching, stating that horses should always take precedence. This resulted in HM Protection Officer (a Chief Inspector) standing to Her Majesty's left and myself immediately to her right. As the lead horse was approaching the group it was apparently 'sparked by the crowd clapping HM' and immediately reared up on its front legs. As the horse came down it kicked the Protection Officer full force in the shoulder, severely injuring same and narrowly missing HM and myself. HM immediately asked the crowd to stop clapping and an ambulance was almost immediately on the scene with Her Majesty personally supervising the patient into the ambulance, making enquiries later in the day regarding the patient's welfare and keeping in close touch with her Protection Officer throughout his long period of sick leave.

HM The Queen is meticulous in observation with a keen sense of humour and a brilliant memory. On one occasion in the mid-nineties Johnny JOHNSON, whilst carrying out his duties as Controller of the Royal Box (he was in fact Operations Director when the Queen was not in attendance), was conveying the Ascot Gold Cup from storage in the main Office Block to the Royal Box when he collided with another object and slightly damaged the cup by inflicting a very small dent thereon. Later in the day whilst handing the Cup to HM Queen for presentation, trying to hide the dent with his gloved hands, HM Queen remarked, "Mr Johnson, before I present that cup again, I suggest it be taken to a Metallurgist for repair."

Towards the end of Johnny JOHNSON's reign at Ascot a very large photograph appeared in a number of Sunday Newspapers showing JOHNSON very much to the fore in the photograph carrying out his duties at Ascot with HM very much in the background.

At the next meeting when HM the Queen was present and about to go on a perambulation from the Royal Box, the Duke of Devonshire, HM the Queen's Representative at Ascot gave the usual warning nod to Johnson on which Johnson took the usual action in warning me.

The entourarge lined up in the normal manner but HM the Queen did not appear with her Representative as expected. There was no sign of Her Majesty in the Royal Box and Johnson did not know her whereabouts, so he made the decision to carry on without her. On arriving at the entrance to the Parade Ring, Johnson suddenly saw HM the Queen coming from his right with a huge grin on her face. Instead of coming out of the main entrance to the Royal Box to join the entourage, she had descended the Fire Escape at the front of the Royal Box, carried on in front of the stands, through the 1,2,3, and out to the Parade Ring. After this incident, right up through my time to the end of the 'Old Course' photographs taken by the' Media' never included the Royal Box Controller.

Towards the end of my period as Manager of the Paddock I was on duty during the 'Royal Week' when the course was hit by a very bad storm, with a large crowd present, consisting of continuous downpours of heavy rain and a very high dangerous wind. The storm got so bad that portable fences, chairs etcetera were flying about in the air, placing the crowd in a very dangerous situation. I immediately gave my staff orders to take all portable fences surrounding bars etc down and to stack the chairs. Shortly after giving the order, the removal of objects in the Paddock was viewed by cameras in the Control Room. As a result twice I was ordered to stop the action at once as it was considered entirely unnecessary.

I ignored both instructions and carried on. The CEO (a retired Army Brigadier with considerable experience in Northern Ireland during the Troubles there) repeated the order in no uncertain terms. I ignored it again. This resulted in the CEO visiting the Paddock in person. When he got to me, having seen the situation for himself, he placed his arms around me and thanked me most profusely. Racing was abandoned.

Circa 1997, after many lucrative offers, I left the Paddock and took over the responsibilities of Manager of Tattersalls, Silver Ring and 66 turnstiles with a staff of over 250. This was a task that I never fully enjoyed, mainly because I was never given sufficient staff to carry out the job. To say the least, keeping a constant eye on a number of Turnstile Operators with very little assistance from the 'Permanent Staff at Ascot' was more or less impossible. The turnstiles had been in existence since the late nineteenth century and being entirely mechanical were maintained by the mechanics of 'Mays Garage' which was situated close by in Winkfield Road. Talking about Mays Garage brings back a past memory when I first joined the Berkshire Constabulary. I had only been stationed at Ascot a few weeks when I was on duty in Ascot High Street when the Fire Brigade (Henry was Chief Fireman) were called to a fire in Sunningdale. On passing the Fire Station I enquired why the engine had not left for the fire. I was told they were one short and invited me to make the number up. En route we had to pass the Police Station when my Sergeant was looking out of the window.

Oh dear, my first disciplinary offence

With crowds up to 70,000 on any one day, Race Managers were kept very busy from the time of arrival on the course at 0800 for briefing right through to departure as late as 1900, when in my case you were faced with a 55-mile journey home. This was certainly the case with regard to my latest responsibility. During my period in this post there were many incidents, far too many to describe. In 2000 I was required to deal with a very embarrassing and difficult incident which occurred on Ladies Day just before the Gold Cup. It came to my notice that the pipes under the Tattersalls Stand had burst, causing sewage etc to come up through the ground surface just south of the stand and run right across the public enclosure to the main entrance to the course. This meant that Racegoers, in all their 'Ladies Day' finery, had to trudge through sewage etc. It was immediately apparent that heavy vehicles to pump up the liquid, take it from the course and then on to a suitable area where it could be deposited were required. Without all the other problems it was a major task to get just one heavy vehicle through the large crowd which would only convey 'a drop from the ocean'. It was therefore necessary for the Ascot Authority Office to obtain a large number of vehicles, some travelling a long distance. The ongoing result was that one vehicle was allowed in the Enclosure at a time which meant it took several hours to disperse the whole amount. Somehow the task was completed without interrupting the racing schedule and without evacuating the course.

After this incident I tendered my resignation, but the Ascot Authority prevailed upon me to remain in post until after the July meeting that year. In 2003 I was asked to return and take over the position of Royal Box Controller/Royal Liaison Officer until the 'Old Course' closed down in late 2004.

Life as Royal Liaison Officer/Controller of Royal Box was very interesting, and many incidents took place during my tenure of the office. It is of course a great privilege to hold such a position which often brought you into personal contact with Her Majesty The Queen and ther members of the Royal Family. Security was such that only persons invited by Her Majesty could be admitted into the area. It is also one of my own personal principles when occupied writing these memoirs that only incidents involving the Royal Family which occurred in full view of the public should be recorded.

REFLECTIONS ON RETIREMENT AFTER 21 YEARS AS A ROYAL BOX STEWARD, GUARDS POLO CLUB

My lifelong interest in Windsor Great Park commenced in May 1952 when as a young Constable with the former Berkshire Constabulary stationed at Ascot I was despatched on my bicycle to support the Windsor Great Park section of the Force in the protection of HM The Queen Mother and HRH Princess Margaret during their periods of residence at Royal Lodge. This interest and the association with 'Royal Protection' was to remain with me for many years, culminating in my being asked to take on the position of 'Royal Liaison Officer/Controller Royal Box' with the Ascot Racecourse Authority.

I well remember the formation of the Guards Polo Club in 1955 and during the period 1974 to 1977 whilst holding the post of Deputy Divisional Commander of the Slough Division of the Thames Valley Police again came into contact with 'Guards' being generally involved within the Division in the preparations for Her Majesty the Queen's Jubilee Celebrations.

Circa 1990 I was approached and asked if I would be interested in becoming a Steward with 'Guards' in view of my experience gained in the Police Service as a Senior Police Officer, and in consequence started my duties towards the end of the reign of Major Ronald Ferguson. On my first day in order that I may settle in, I was given the task of 'Keeping the Polo Lines' sterile. Whilst I was carrying out this task I was greatly impressed with the manner in which Major

Ferguson ensured that the whole operation was organised with such great military precision that every part functioned like a 'well oiled machine'. During the morning I was also amazed to witness the arrival of the late Kerry Packer's five vehicle convoy.

At that time a former member of the 'Household Cavalry' whom I had previously met as a member of the Special Constabulary in Windsor, known generally as Ginger, was also employed as a Steward mainly on vehicle parking and crowd control. Ginger certainly was a character and well known for his 'plain and direct speaking' when carrying out his duties. Such was his personality that he quickly came to the attention of HRH The Prince of Wales, who on one occasion after a visit to the United States of America presented Ginger with a cowboy hat and boots, which Ginger always wore when carrying out his duties, much to the amusement of all in attendance including the members of the Royal Family.

On my second day on duty I was duly appointed as a Steward in the Royal Box, a post I greatly enjoyed until Cartier International Day on 24th July 2011 when I decided to 'hang up my well polished Oxford shoes' and enter final retirement pending my 80th birthday in September.

Looking back over the past 21 years with 'Guards', two main changes come quickly to mind, namely the change of status of the Club from a 'Military Organisation' to a 'Civilian Organisation' some years ago and the recent re-building of premises which has brought about a magnificent centre worthy of the 'Guards Polo Club'. Before the change in status International Cartier Day was organised very much in a 'Military' manner. Many of the Stewards present had experienced service in the armed forces and therefore tended to carry out their duties with military precision. Rehearsals were regularly held early in the day under the supervision of the Chairman to ensure that all went to time and according to tradition later. One Chairman always inspected in detail the Royal Box and surrounds and would order that any dust etc on the site and the slightest algae which had formed on a post, be removed at once. Over the years after the change of status, the general situation has become more relaxed, the Chairman, Chief Executive Officer and Head Steward briefing that all Stewards should display a cheerful countenance towards the public, be approachable at all times and deal with any problem that may arise in a sympathetic manner, thus creating a very happy and enjoyable atmosphere throughout the day. This desired situation has been achieved and the younger stewards who have not experienced military service have fitted in very well.

FREEMASONRY – SUCCESS
OR DISAPPOINTMENT

In August 1948, owing to my 'Father's Apparent Misdeeds' in dealing with the wastage 'School Dinners' at East Ilsley School during the period 1944 to 1947 which resulted in a sudden move from East Ilsley to the 'Wilds of Wiltshire' within days, I suddenly found myself without employment and residence I could consider 'home'. My mother's sister Aunty May quickly came to the rescue (with certain conditions) regarding a 'home' and the Berkshire Constabulary kindly arranged for Cadet 10 Allen to be moved from Newbury to Wokingham.

I now go back to the year 1926 when my father and mother married. My father having been brought up in Crowthorne and educated at Ranelagh School, Bracknell (the only Church Grammar School within the Oxford Diocese) was still in contact with many close friends he attended school with. A number of these friends later became members of the Downshire Lodge at Wokingham and my father had in fact agreed to join them. My mother apparently (just before her marriage) 'put her foot down' and said "No we cannot afford such an expensive luxury" and this was the end of his intention. In later years this decision was regretted which was duly noted by his intended 'Proposer and Seconder' to the Lodge.

During my period at Crowthorne and throughout my 'National Service' these 'friends' gradually prepared me to become a Mason and by the time I had left the army the necessary forms had been completed and the long wait to join began. In February 1953 I received a letter advising me to report to the Wokingham Masonic Hall on 15th February 1953 for 'Initiation', a date which was most convenient for me as I was scheduled for 0600 to 1400 hours duty at Ascot. On 13th February 1953 Sergeant Reginald Haines changed my duties to 1400 to 2200 hours for no apparent reason. I duly informed the Downshire Lodge I was unable to attend. The next day my Chief Inspector (Evans) instructed that I be returned to my original duties for 15th February without explanation. The Initiation took place but a few days later I was at the usual 'Morning Coffee Break' in the Single Quarters at Ascot when a Detective Constable brought to the notice of all present that I had become a Freemason, in rather derogative terms. The announcement met with uproar almost leading to 'fisticuffs'. I quickly realised that I had possibly made a wrong decision but carried on with the project.

I soon found there were advantages such as turning a 'shy young chap' into a very confident person who was able to stand up and make a speech with no problems at all and soldiered on through the various offices in the lodge reaching the position of Worshipful Master in 1966 whilst stationed at Wallingford as a Country Sergeant. A coach load of supporters from Wallingford actually travelled to Wokingham to support my elevation. I also joined a number of other lodges in various degrees and found myself soon carrying out the offices of either Secretary, Treasurer or Director of Ceremonies in them. Sadly on having been persuaded to take over as Treasurer in some instances I came across problems left by the previous occupant of the office such as failing to get all annual subscriptions in on time and producing 'Annual Financial Statements' which lacked sufficient details of expenditure. In one case on taking over the books I found that many members, some of high rank, were in arrears with subscriptions for as long as two years. This of course was before the age of the computers when normally the Treasurer would send a personal letter in each case. As there was a large number involved, I took the liberty of typing out a wax stencil, duplicating same and forwarding the same in the form of a circular to all involved, including members of Grand and Provincial Grand Rank status. This action caused great indignation in the case of the more 'Senior Masons' for which today over forty years later I am still not forgiven; in fact, on submitting my resignation which became necessary as I was tending my very sick wife as a full time carer, it was not even acknowledged in any way despite the intervention of the Provincial Grand Master on my behalf. I had also previously resigned from a Chapter after 42 years' loyal service in all offices including Provincial. Result – one line from Secretary 'Your resignation is noted – the return of your regalia would be appreciated'.

In the 1980/1990s I became a Founder of a number of lodges, held positions such as 'Founder Director of Ceremonies' and 'Treasurer' in some and rose to the rank of Provincial Senior Warden in a Province. Sadly during the year of office, the Provincial Grand Master died and his successor was taken seriously ill with cancer, which meant I was continually representing the Provincial Grand Master on every occasion – a very demanding year for me.

During 1989 I was appointed Founder Director of Ceremonies of a Mark Lodge of M.M.M. and with great enthusiasm I went about my duties as such. After the first few meetings I found that because no 'Lodge of Instruction' had been held before the actual meeting, chaos was present on my arrival at every meeting caused by acting Officers not being present and no arrangements for the vacancy to be filled on the night. There was also hesitation during the ceremonies for the same reason. I therefore pleaded with the 'Executive of the Lodge' that 'Lodges of Instruction' were very necessary. This met with a blank refusal on the grounds that the Senior Officers of the Province who had been appointed to acting office in this lodge could carry out their working with perfection without. I immediately resigned from the lodge. Sometime later I was invited back to the lodge as a guest but unfortunately on arrival I was asked to take over a vacant office without any notice. At the Festive Board at this particular meeting the Provincial Grand Master whilst on his feet making a speech remarked, "We do welcome back to the lodge this evening W. Bro. Richard ALLEN but it was noted that he was having problems with his signs in that he did not know where his heart was. Still being a former Police Officer he would not have a heart". I later spoke to the dear gentleman and pointed out my neck and shoulders were riddled with arthritis making life difficult. I did not receive any form of apology. Years later I experienced the same problem in another degree when the head of that degree made a similar remark. I never went to another meeting in that degree.

Circa 1980 I had joined a Degree meeting in the Oxfordshire Masonic Centre. I later went through all the offices eventually finishing up as Secretary which turned out to be a very onerous task throughout in that later I would be faced with many problems concerning the 'Management of 333'. Until then I had only good memories of the organisation, my first memory going back to an excellent manager whose father and he were greatly respected members of a lodge in Wallingford. This manager was followed by a great friend of his who was also very competent and honest. During this period of my Masonic Life I experienced the following problems with 333:

On at least two occasions we were forced to dine on the landing instead of the Dining Room owing to 'double booking'.

On one occasion we were granted a room on the ground floor to change into our regalia.

When we retired from the lodge room we found that all our clothing plus wallets and other personal items had been moved from the room occupied to a heap on the cellar floor without any protection or prior notice whatsoever.

(c) At a Rotary Meeting I was approached by a member of the 333 Committee. He stated that 333 were experiencing financial problems and were looking for a way to increase income, one being letting about twenty spaces in 333 Car Park. At that time he was aware that a neighbouring garage was experiencing parking problems and that I could help. The Garage Manager was approached and an agreement signed. All went well for about three weeks until 333 upset their neighbour over smoke from 333's barbecue. The neighbour complained to the Oxford City Planning Officer whilst playing either golf or bowls. The Planning Officer stated that Planning Laws were being broken. Immediately 333 cancelled the agreement without any notice whatsoever leaving the Garage Manager 'high and dry' without any compensation or for that matter any apology.

When 333 raised the rent for the lodge this caused a considerable rise in subscriptions causing 15 members to resign on the spot. I eventually found accommodation at Woodstock Masonic Hall at a much lower rent, but the senior members of the Province who also were members of the lodge voted against the proposition and in consequence I also resigned from the office of Secretary and the lodge.

After I left 333 the management of the centre greatly deteriorated leading to the whole building and grounds being sold, in many members' opinion undersold, which led to lodge meetings being held in marquees at back of hotels etcetera.

Looking back in retirement I now realise I should have retired from the Force in August 1981 when l first had 30 years' service to my credit (29 years 6 months + 6 months from my Cadet Days). I had at one stage decided to retire with 25 years' service but was unable to obtain suitable employment at the time. I have regretted this decision ever since.

1981-1984 proved very difficult for me through no fault of my own. In August 1981 I was President of the Officers Mess Committee and had been since 1978. Peter Imbert was settling in as Chief Constable and very anxious to meet anybody of standing who would propel him back to the Metropolitan Police for further promotion. With great charm he relied on his Senior Officers to run the Force with him and endeavoured to be very popular at all times both with members of the Force and the local public. At an HQ Officers Dinner he prevailed upon me to approach a guest, who happened to be the Duke of Kent's Personal Secretary, to ask him whether The Duke of Kent (Grand Master of England Freemasonry) would be willing to attend the next Dinner which would be held at Sulhamstead. The Duke of Kent accepted the invitation and many other 'Civil Dignitaries' also attended. A few weeks afterwards I was asked to ascertain whether the Duke of Marlborough would like to follow suit at a dinner to be held at Windsor. On the day of the Dinner at Windsor, a great friend and respected colleague of many years and myself received information from the Chief Constable that Chief Superintendent JONES (Ex Gloucestershire and at the time Divisional Commander of Newbury Division) was to be 'Short Tracked' on the instructions of the Home Office to the Metropolitan Police for 'promotion' via Oxford and ACC Kidlington. The Dinner took place although the Duke of Marlborough was one hour late and the meal was put back accordingly. From that event onwards l noticed a sharp change in the Chief Constable's attitude towards me – it went from friendly to almost hostile overnight for apparently no reason.

Shortly after this revelation, a journalist, who was also a member of the Thames Valley Police Committee, wrote a controversial article headed 'The Police and Freemasonry' which was published in the Oxford Weekly Times. The article named in 'Banner Headlines' three Chief Superintendents of Thames Valley Police, namely myself and two colleagues. Two of us took no action and the third to whom the insinuations were more direct resigned from Freemasonry immediately, a move quite understandable as he had only been a Freemason for a very short period. I was never questioned on this matter by any member of the force or the Thames Valley Police Authority.

After this the Chief Constable came to me with a date for the AGM of the HQ Officers Mess. The date was not suitable for me to attend as I would be in Spain. Despite my requesting that the date be changed, the Chief Constable arranged for the meeting to take place. When I returned, l found I had been replaced as PMC by a respected colleague.

On 1st November 1982 I was relieved of my command of the Traffic Division without notice and posted to Banbury as Divisional Commander of the Banbury Division. The Chief Constable rarely came to Banbury to see me and this applied even when I was running a Division with virtually no officers on patrol owing to many being committed to policing the miners striking in the North of England.

During my time at Banbury I applied for two Civilian Posts within TVP namely Civilian Administrative Officer for Oxford Division and a similar post at Headquarters. Both went to Chief Inspectors already in post on retirement. I might add at this stage that l had carried out similar duties during my service and received promotion onwards relatively soon afterwards. The Chief Constable, however, let it be known in the Force that I had not got the jobs because the Thames Valley Police Authority had barred serving officers from taking up such employment on retirement. To my knowledge I was the only person ever barred.

I did not realise the significance of my falling out of favour with Peter Imbert until I read of his death and obituary in the Guardian Newspaper many years later, which in effect stated that he would always be remembered for endeavouring to abolish Freemasonry from the Metropolitan Police Force.

I later went through the chairs of the Buttercross Lodge in 2010 and the Jersey Lodge in 2013 before becoming an Honorary Member of the Downshire Lodge in 2019.

Appraisal

Looking back I consider I should have left being involved in Freemasonry two or three years until I was more mature and considering matrimony. During the period I was at Bracknell I coped with Freemasonry well and whilst at Abingdon, Wallingford and Bracknell (second time) found it most worthwhile and supportive for many reasons. When I eventually moved to Witney and having joined a number of 'Side Degrees' on the way, I came to suspect that Freemasonry was changing and this like many other 'walks of life' through a lack 'Military Type Discipline'. From the time I joined in 1953 when Provincial Grand Masters had been and still were Lieutenant Colonels (Rtd) and other high ranking personage with excellent 'Management Skills' to 2018 when the standard had lowered in many instances to persons with virtually no 'Management Experience'. This led to many persons joining Freemasonry with virtually no leadership or Management experience, gaining positions where they were delighted to exhibit power and influence and gain apparently high positions within Freemasonry. In order to keep up the numbers joining, vetting standards were lowered to accept persons with very little knowledge of their background and suitability to become masons. I can remember a number of masons who, once in, developed criminal tendencies within the order, committed offences, but apart from being forced to resign entirely escaped court appearances because it was policy not to report any such matters to the police in the first place. I must state that one of the finest Provincial Grand Masters of Berkshire I had the great pleasure to serve under was the late Brigadier E.W.C. Flavell DSO, MC,TD,DL who held the position from 1967 to 1985, who was followed by John H.W. Wilder CSE.BA. who was another fine man who had been 'Commissioned' in the army, whom I knew well, especially as he was my next door neighbour at Wallingford and who also took, together with his wife, a great interest in my progression through the 'Police Ranks' long after I had left Wallingford, which of course was much appreciated.

I must state that the problems I have described above also, in my opinion, are present within 'Rotary International' (member for 36 years – five clubs, namely, Wallingford, Bracknell, Caversham, Slough, Oxford North and Windrush Valley). Even in 'Probus' changes are being noticed now owing to the fact that many members have not experienced any form of 'Armed Services' life. Sixty years ago, you could not join Freemasonry without two 'References' from long-standing acquaintances/friends, an 'In Depth Interview' followed by a wait of up to three years. In Rotary you had to be invited to join, be 'Head' of your business/Profession in the area covered by the Club, and subject also to an 'In Depth Interview'. To become a 'District Governor' you had to be very distinguished and well able in the arts of 'Public Speaking' and 'Management'.

Over recent years a practice of advertising for prospective members for both organisations has crept in owing mainly to the fact the organisations may be unable to retain their membership as a result of falling standards.

To sum up, I experienced many happy years to start with but when standards of discipline started to deteriorate generally throughout the country, I began to see a great change in the standards of discipline within Freemasonry in too many respects to list. I regret to say that if the decline continues there may be no such organisation in existence in ten years' time.

'A potent masonic memory'

Having celebrated my 53rd year in Craft Freemasonry in February 2006, I can recall many memorable events such as the Investiture of HRH The Duke of Kent as Grand Master in the Albert Hall, London in 1967, which I had the privilege to attend being the WM of the Downshire Lodge that year. One event circa 1968, however, frequently comes to mind when considering the ethics of Freemasonry.

I, together with two other guests, were invited by a Past Master of the Pangbourne Lodge resident in Cholsey, Berkshire to attend his 'London Lodge' which met at 'The Four Horse Shoes, Tottenham Court Road on a Saturday afternoon commencing at 2.30pm. The summons stated that a second degree ceremony would start the meeting, followed by an Initiation and the Festive Board at which 'regalia would be worn'. We had been told by our host that the WM would be initiating his son at this, the last meeting of his year as WM.

The meeting was extremely well attended and all guests received a very warm welcome. The WM carried out the second degree in a first-class manner, after which we were 'called off' for tea. Before leaving the temple, however, he warned all present that if anyone noticed anything untoward during the break no comment should be made under any circumstances.

After the Lodge was 'called on' there was a strange silence throughout. Knocks were received on the door and it was announced that a certain Past Master was seeking admission. Immediately the Past Master's name was announced, many present were obviously very surprised if not shocked. The Past Master was admitted in a wheelchair dressed in his pyjamas, dressing gown and full masonic regalia. It was quite obvious he was very ill. He was wheeled towards the 'Chair' and the WM announced that he would not be initiating his own son as stated in the summons on this occasion as the Past Master would be initiating his son and in consequence handed over the gavel. The Past Master's son was completely unaware of the situation and was of the opinion that his father was very ill in hospital suffering from terminal cancer. He had, however, been warned to attend the Lodge at short notice thinking that the WM would be carrying out the ceremony. The look on the son's face when he heard his father's voice for the first time in the Lodge will never leave me. The Past Master conducted the whole ceremony in an impeccable manner. Immediately after he had completed the actual ceremony, he was conveyed back to hospital in a waiting ambulance where he died some ten days later.

Printed in Great Britain
by Amazon

17467442R00108